"The Church of the Wild movement is one of the most exciting advances in spirituality since Franciscan, Sufi, and Kabbalah mystics entertained dialogues with one another in Spain six centuries ago. But like any rewarding trip into the wilderness, you need a good field guide. Not only will this book reenergize your own faith, but it can help you build a stronger local community through creative liturgies and inspiring insights. It is a keeper."

—**Gary Paul Nabhan**, author of *Jesus for Farmers and Fishers* and other books

"*Field Guide to Church of the Wild* is an indispensable resource for starting and nurturing church in the wild. A feast of rituals, stories, and wisdom, this book inspires and invites us into the practice of reconnecting, re-storying, and restoring wild spirituality with humans and more-than-humans. A must-have companion to *Church of the Wild*!"

—**Su Yon Pak**, coauthor of *Sisters in Mourning* and dean at Union Theological Seminary

"I had hoped that this *Field Guide to Church of the Wild* would give you practical, step-by-step instructions for forming and guiding a church of the wild. The authors actually give you something so much better—living examples of what people are actually doing right now in wild churches around the world. Be careful: as you read this book, you might just feel both an invitation and empowerment to bring some people together in an outdoor spiritual adventure."

—**Brian D. McLaren**, author of *Do I Stay Christian?* and *Life After Doom*

"This valuable guide offers an abundance of simple but profound practices and experiments for recalling, reconnecting with, and appreciating the sacred dimension of the natural world. These places of reconnection reveal an emerging story of our passage as a species from an artificial state of exile into our birthright of earthly homecoming. This is exactly the kind of guidance we need to mature and deepen our relations with our mistreated but vitally animate world even while building inclusive relationships with one another."

—**Craig Chalquist**, PhD, author of *Terrapsychological Inquiry* and coeditor of *Ecotherapy: Healing with Nature in Mind*

"*Field Guide to Church of the Wild* includes a treasure trove of ecospiritual practices and resources generously offered by a diverse group of wise, experienced leaders. Wrapped in the inspiring prose of Victoria Loorz and Valerie Luna Serrels, this book holds the potential to deepen and enrich the work of all those committed to deeper relationship with this sacred Earth."

—**Leah Rampy**, author of *Earth and Soul: Reconnecting amid Climate Chaos*; coauthor of *Discovering the Spiritual Wisdom of Trees*; founder and guide, Church of the Wild Two Rivers

"In the long years when I was a Methodist Sunday school teacher, we met outdoors as often as in—because that is where it felt most natural to understand the God of creation. This beautiful book will help many to make that lovely and powerful connection."

—**Bill McKibben**, author of *The End of Nature* and other books

"I highly recommend this invaluable resource for anyone wishing to start a church of the wild and develop a deep, sustained connection with nature and Spirit. Drawn from years of the authors' own experience as well as that of a number of Church of the Wild leaders, the book is not only chock-full of practical resources, rituals, and practices; it also provides a rich spiritual grounding for these gatherings."

—**Beth Norcross,** founding director of The Center
for Spirituality in Nature, coauthor of *Discovering
the Spiritual Wisdom of Trees*

Field Guide to Church of the Wild

Field Guide to
Church of
the Wild

Victoria Loorz and
Valerie Luna Serrels

Broadleaf Books
Minneapolis

29 28 27 26 25 24   1 2 3 4 5 6 7 8 9

Illustrations by Manne Green [mannegreen.art]

Interior design by Olivia Loorz [olivialoorz.com]

Library of Congress Cataloging-in-Publication Data

Names: Loorz, Victoria, author. | Serrels, Valerie Luna, author.
Title: Field guide to church of the wild / Victoria Loorz and Valerie Serrels.
Description: Minneapolis : Broadleaf Books, [2025] | Contains bibliographical references.
Identifiers: LCCN 2024014508 | ISBN 9781506496351 (print) | ISBN
   9781506496399 (ebook)
Subjects: LCSH: Nature—Religious aspects—Christianity. | Human
   ecology—Religious aspects—Christianity.
Classification: LCC BT695.5 .L667 2025 | DDC 261.8/8—dc23/eng/20240708
LC record available at https://lccn.loc.gov/2024014508

Cover design by Laura Drew

Print ISBN: 978-1-5064-9635-1
eBook ISBN: 978-1-5064-9639-9

*To all Wild Church leaders, lands, and
lineages who weave together this movement,
with fierce love for its continued unfolding.
May we be the ancestors who continue the ancient thread,
living in reverence and reciprocity with the creatures,
elements, green growing beings, landscapes, stars,
and heavenly bodies. Amen.*

CONTENTS

1 *Wild Church: An Emergence* **1**

2 *Getting Started: The Ways of Wild Leadership* **13**

3 *Arrival: Grounding in Sacred Presence* **35**

4 *Ancestral Reverence: Acknowledging the Land's Story* **49**

5 *Wild Rituals: Re-Placing Liturgy, Stories, and Prayers* **65**

6 *Earth Cycles: Reorienting to the Rhythm of the Wild* **87**

7 *Conversation with the Holy Wild: Solo Sauntering as Sermon* **101**

8 *Re-Storying Our Place: Sharing in Circle* **117**

9 *Offerings and Benediction: Practicing Wild Reciprocity* **129**

Field Notes for Creating a Wild Church **139**

Gratitudes and Connections **150**

Contributors **151**

Notes **161**

ANATOMY OF A WILD CHURCH

1 *Emergence*
2 *Leadership*
3 *Grounding*
4 *Stories*
5 *Rituals*
6 *Cycles*
7 *Sauntering*
8 *Sharing*
9 *Reciprocity*

All epigraphs come from Victoria Loorz, *Church of the Wild: How Nature Invites Us Into the Sacred* (Minneapolis: Broadleaf Books, 2021).

1
WILD CHURCH
An Emergence

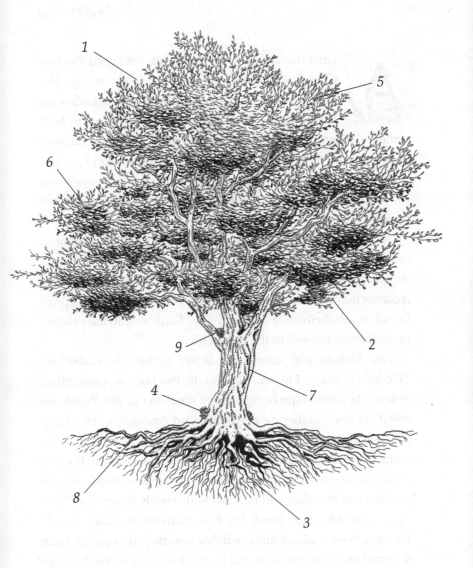

"The time has come to . . . return to intimate relationship with the living world. More and more of us are taking our place, once again, as full participants in the web of life, which we remember is held together by love."

—*Church of the Wild*

 large oak tree in Ojai, California, beckoned the first Church of the Wild into existence a few years ago. Her broad and inviting canopy and sturdy branches offered a sanctuary as magnificent as any human-built cathedral. There, a small group gathered to embody spiritual practices that helped them fall in love with a suffering world . . . and they called it church. It was the beginning of a movement you can read about in *Church of the Wild: How Nature Invites Us into the Sacred*.

Church of the Wild, practiced as a personal spirituality or in communion with other people, is more than a novel way to do church outside. It is an emerging yet ancient spiritual practice of reconnection with the rest of the living world as kin. It is a practice of re-sacralizing our wild and alive Earth and, in the process, remembering our role in the web of life.

We, Victoria and Valerie—or, as our mother often called us, "Vic-Val . . . Val . . . I mean, Vic!"—write this book as a joint effort of love. As sisters who moved many times in our childhood, we relied on one another as playmates and confidants. As adults, we have deepened our friendship through our spiritual journeys, which always seem to align. Sometimes one of us will call the other and share some insight or discovery we've been pondering for months, and the other will respond with sisterly things like "Shut up . . . get out of my head! *I've* been thinking the same thing!" We have been walking this rewilding church path together since it started over a decade ago, and together we have worked to support the growing movement.

After twenty years as a pastor of what I (Victoria) now call *indoor churches*, I walked out the chapel doors and into the sanctuary of oak trees. For years, I'd kept my experience of the Sacred in the natural world separate from both my professional church leadership and my climate activism. That separation led to deep burnout. Eventually, I realized that the severance of my spirituality from the very geography of my most numinous experiences of God was the problem itself. Moving church outside, under the branches of a giant oak tree—listening for whispers of divine presence in the wind, through the calls of crows and mockingbirds, and in the buzz of gnats—offered me a pathway of reconnection, which is the core meaning of religion. I found, through creating Church of the Wild, a way to re-pair my spirituality with nature: a wild spirituality of radical belonging to the whole sacred interconnected world.

I (Valerie) had been coming home from church each Sunday feeling depressed and disconnected. Instead of feeling a sense of community with others or a sense of the Holy, I felt adrift and alone. Eventually, I was no longer willing to try to fit into a theology and way of understanding self, church, and the world that no longer felt right. I could feel something new was emerging, but it remained unknown. I left church, but the sense of disconnection didn't shift. Only when I started a Church of the Wild in Virginia and began to embody practices that offered a deeper connection with Earth and Spirit did I realize that the intimate human community I was yearning for was happening. I didn't realize that the ducks in my front yard and the sparrows and soil were part of that community until I included them in my spiritual story.

THE WILD CHURCH MOVEMENT

The Wild Church Network was launched after a group of thirty or so spiritual leaders from multiple denominations of the Christ tradition got together after quietly creating their own versions

4

of wild church. We all had separately realized that we needed to stop trying to fix church as it is and start experimenting with what church could be. Moving outside of buildings, we were creating something more than simply "doing church outside." With different influences and coming from diverse traditions, we were fascinated to discover that what we were creating separately was remarkably aligned. For example, almost all of us, without checking with one another, included a time of solo wandering or sacred sauntering. During this time, we invited our little wild congregations to contemplatively connect with the trees, stones, creeks, and wild beings of our places and return to share with others. Our shared desire was to stop simply talking *about* God and to offer opportunities for people to encounter God directly in nature.

When the *Church of the Wild* book was released a few years later, we were afraid it would be too Christian for not-Christians and too not-Christian for Christians. That it would appeal to exactly nobody. We were wrong. Turns out there are *lots* of people walking along the edges of their religious identity, no matter what it is, and wrestling with a great longing to make their faith wild again, to reconnect their spirituality with the rest of the living world.

Though wild church began within the Christ tradition, it quickly became clear that the gatherings attracted nonsectarian, interreligious, and nonreligious communions of people. While some wild church communities identify as explicitly Christian, interspiritual, Buddhist, or spiritual but not religious, the common invitation is to rewild your spirituality, no matter what your tradition or orientation. Wild church doesn't ask people to leave or join any particular religion. The us-them boundaries of religious identity are less important than the common roots of our shared belonging with a sacred Earth.

Over the past decade, we have witnessed the seeds of this movement germinate into something beyond anything we expected.

Since the inception of the network, many more wild churches have continued to pop up like mushrooms throughout North America and other Western nations. It is as if the seeds of our ancestors, whose spiritualities at one point in history or another were deeply connected with place, are sprouting through us. Earth-based, place-rooted spirituality has been the norm throughout most of human history, as is seen in Indigenous cultures throughout the world today.

We thought we were making things up at first; we had just started doing what our hearts were longing for: creating spiritual practices to reconnect with Earth as sacred. Once we met and started sharing our stories, though, we realized we were part of something larger than us: a work of the Spirit, a zeitgeist of an emerging consciousness that Earth herself seemed to be initiating. We built a website and named what was happening a "network." Only then were we able to see the larger picture: our little gatherings are part of a larger movement of an important emerging story, one that is helping to shift a worldview of dominance into a worldview of kindred interconnection.

EMERGENCE OF A KINDER WORLD
Systems theorist Margaret Wheatley debunks the idea that the world changes incrementally, one person at a time. Rather, she shows that social innovations scale to impact the trajectory of a society in the same way evolutionary change happens in any ecosystem: through a process she calls *emergence*. Hints of change may glow on the edges for a while, but at a critical point, the world changes. And it happens when "constant interactions among individuals suddenly coalesce to create something new and different," which is exactly what is happening with the emergence of wild church.

Wheatley explains that this kind of networking extends the influence of the movement to a greater scale. The system itself, rather than any strategic efforts of networking organizations, is what mysteriously influences the wider society beyond what any of the individual churches could do on their own.

Most surprising and hopeful is the understanding that when a new value system, worldview, or cultural behavior is ready to emerge, it will. And nothing can stop it. Those of us who are long- ing for a new way of relating to nature and Spirit become part of the emergence, but we aren't controlling it. Resistance to the emergence—fighting back by the status quo—will occur. But since emergence is the result of the collaborative, interconnected webs of relationships that created it, worldviews shift despite (or per- haps because of) the resistance. Baking soda, sugar, and flour ar- en't a cookie, but the interconnection of them, with the addition of heat, creates a cookie, something totally new. At that point, it can't be unbaked.

Or, as Paul Kingsnorth puts it, "The dead leaves of one culture fall to cover the seeds of another, already sown beneath. The more things fall apart—the more the centre cannot hold—the more new centres are seeded on the margins, which is the only place they can ever grow."

What we are witnessing in the emergence of a movement to restore sacred relationship with Earth is something larger than wild church. It is a signal to us that a kinship worldview is emerg- ing. Any loud resistance to that emergence will not prevail.

CONSEQUENCES OF A WORLDVIEW OF DISCONNECTION

The wild church movement is rising at a profound turning point in history. Our planetary ecosystems are in crisis. It is critical for people of all faiths to repair our severed relationships with Earth.

The primary public narrative of the climate emergency, even within religious communities, is overwhelmingly political, tech- nological, and scientific. A focus on shifting from fossil fuels to renewable energy, for example, is absolutely essential. The underlying spiritual shift is rarely addressed, however, even within religious circles. A false duality has sunk deep into our vocabulary, culture, and worldview: we think of nature as something *out there*, separate from humans, available for our use and enjoyment. And this false belief system of human supremacy and dominance is a serious spiritual problem. Severing our spirituality from the natural world allows us to desacralize what is inherently holy. We abuse what we no longer consider sacred. And the Earth suffers greatly for it.

What is less obvious, but equally dangerous, are the psychospiritual consequences suffered by our own species. A spirituality rooted in human superiority—like any form of othering and supremacy—is detrimental to the whole system. As Sufi mystic and author Llewellyn Vaughan-Lee shares, "The world is not a problem to be solved; it is a living being to which we belong. The world is part of our own self and we are a part of its suffering wholeness. Until we go to the root of our image of separateness, there can be no healing. And the deepest part of our separateness from creation lies in our forgetfulness of its sacred nature, which is also our own sacred nature."

What do our souls lose by forgetting that we are part of nature? What is atrophied in our spiritual reality when we pretend we are the only species who really matters to God? Human attachment with God, when disconnected from the land and placed instead in the sky or within a building, not only desacralizes the land; it diminishes the capacity of the human soul to live into the sacred story of love and reconciliation at the heart of every religious tradition.

A NEW STORY IS EMERGING

We don't pretend that we know what is emerging. Mostly, it is about living with and into the questions. But we do know this. What is needed now is a way of relating to the world beyond creation care, which is still rooted in a hierarchy of superiority, as if we humans are the ones who know what is needed to make the necessary shifts of survival. What's ultimately required is a change of heart, a shift in how we relate to each other and to the whole of the living Earth. It is a shift from stewardship to relationship. And this is inherently spiritual work.

The wisdom we need for this time of great unraveling will be gained as we remember that we are not separate from nature. The voices we need to listen most closely to at this time are the voices that the dominant culture has overlooked, dismissed, ignored, or silenced. The voices of Indigenous peoples who have never forgotten our place in the web of belonging. The voices of women, of communities of color, of those from the queer community who have suffered the impact of a dominant culture of supremacy for generations. Voices from the Southern Hemisphere, from religions outside our comfort zone whose perspectives are essential to even see our own blindness. The voices of the trees, the storms, the cicadas, the rivers, and the tiny viruses whose interconnected suffering and resiliency is essential in this time of dramatic change. The wisdom we need at this pivotal time in our history will be found there, outside the edges of the dominant culture. And by *listening*, we mean practicing kinship, intentionally entering into relationship, through respectful and authentic conversation and presence.

This kinship is at the core of wild church. Kinship is recognizing that our beloved community includes the whole, alive, interconnected world. Wild church is an opportunity to live into that intimate kinship with other beings and, in doing so, to reclaim our own wildness, which is another word for *essence, true self, wholeness*. It is falling in love again with the world, considering the well-being of all the sacred others in our decisions. It is taking on the suffering of our beloveds and engaging in their healing. It is an embodiment of a Hebrew concept known as *tikkun olam*, which means "repairing the world"—the whole world.

As we learn the language of leaves and the banter of berries and then share these little moments of poetic wisdom with one another, we are re-storying our place. We are creating new stories that can guide us into a new and yet ancient way of being human. Re-storying our relationship with the land through spiritual practices like the ones shared in this book is a pathway of restoration as important as planting trees and restoring prairies. Re-storying our relationship with Earth as sacred kin provides a spiritual and emotional foundation of belonging we need to support all the layers of work ahead of us.

A DOGMA-FREE FIELD GUIDE

This book is a field guide to prayers and mountains, rituals and wrens, gatherings and forests, community and mycelial connection. It is a collection of stories and ideas in support of a growing field of practice we call *wild church*, a companion to Victoria's book *Church of the Wild*. Organized around the interconnected parts of an oak tree, each chapter offers stories and spiritual practices related to different components common to many wild churches.

You won't find a list of dogmatic how-tos in this book. Dogs are more welcome than dogma at a church of the wild. It is an emerging field of practice, which means it is still becoming. To codify wild church would kill it, much like what happens when you try to help butterflies struggling to release from their cocoon. If you rush them, they will die. Rather than a *how-to*, each chapter offers stories, ideas, prayers, and practices from a handful of the 250-plus wild churches now blooming in the world. We are learning from one another as we go.

Imagine while you are reading that you are sitting around a campfire in a circle of oak trees as stories are shared. There is laughter and drumming as well as tears and shared grief at a world unraveling. There are moments of holy awe when we realize together that we are part of something much larger than any one of us.

HOW TO READ THIS BOOK

It is no coincidence that Church of the Wild began under a mature oak tree. Turns out human spirituality and oak trees share a long companionship. A staple source of food, fuel, medicine, art, and shelter for early humans before the development of agriculture, the oak tree has been regarded as the sacred tree of life in many places since the late Neolithic period. Oaks are still revered in many cultures, associated with divinity, resilience, and wisdom. With respect for this relationship, the illustrations at the start of each chapter playfully suggest a taxonomy of a *Quercus agrifolia*, or a California live oak, as a structure for common elements of a wild church gathering.

The first two chapters of this field guide offer an introduction to the emerging wild church movement, hints toward a post-patriarchal form of leadership, and describes the role wild church plays in an emerging new story of interconnection and kinship.

The remaining chapters reflect elements of a gathering that we've observed are most common while working with hundreds of wild churches over the past decade. These are practices that can be embodied in your individual contemplative spirituality or in the context of coming together with like-hearted others. They begin with grounding, as a way to orient yourself within a particular place, and include ideas for land acknowledgments, rituals, prayers, and invocations. At the core of a wild church gathering is a time of solo wandering, or sauntering in nature, before coming back together to share insights or experiences. The final chapter looks at how offerings and benedictions take on a new meaning in the context of a beloved community beyond our own species.

In the back of the book is a section we call "Field Notes," which can guide you as you envision the particular version of a wild church that wants to take shape in your home ecosystem.

And so this field guide is an offering of little twigs of stories and practices, which you can collect as tinder to light the fire for your own vision of a Church of the Wild. Wild church is something you can't just read about. You need to experience it yourself: in your own ecosystem, in relationship with your particular community of humans and trees and rivers and hawks and bumblebees. We offer you many wild blessings as you consider the possibilities.

2
GETTING STARTED
The Ways of Wild Leadership

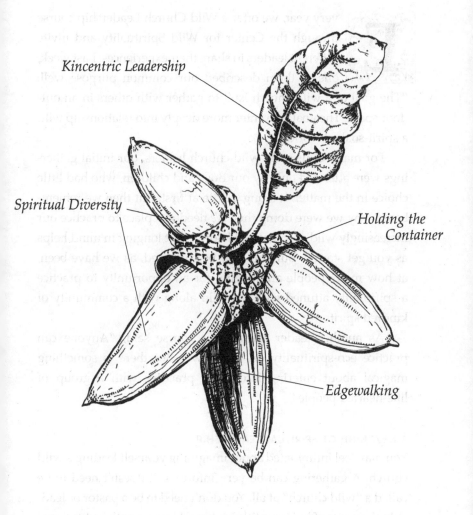

Kincentric Leadership

Spiritual Diversity

Holding the Container

Edgewalking

14

"The well-worn path—the way others have gone—leads you to a place where you are uniquely invited to step off the trail. This is an invitation to depart from what is familiar and easy in order to step into what is wild and unknown."

—*Church of the Wild*

very year, we offer a Wild Church Leadership course through the Center for Wild Spirituality and invite different leaders to share their experiences. Last week, one of them described our common purpose well: "The goal of a wild church isn't to gather with others in an outdoor space. The goal is to enter more deeply into relationship with a spirit-soaked world."

For many of us early wild church leaders, our initial gatherings were attended only by our dogs and children, who had little choice in the matter. It stung a little at first. But then we remembered why we were doing this. We needed a place to practice our increasingly wild spirituality. Holding that longing in mind helps as you get started. But you may be surprised, as we have been, at how many people are longing for an opportunity to practice a spirituality attuned with the wild along with a community of kindred spirits.

As another leader during our course said, "Anyone can practice eco-spirituality on their own. But there is something magical about entering into these practices with a group of like-hearted people."

A NEW KIND OF SPIRITUAL LEADERSHIP

You may feel intimidated about imagining yourself leading a wild church. A gathering can be very informal. It doesn't need to be called a "wild church" at all. You don't need to be a pastor or leader in the sense of having a title bestowed on you with institutional credentials. Rather, your leadership is needed to simply hold the space and invite people to enter into embodied conversation with the Sacred for themselves. There is nothing you need to *make happen*. As a wild church leader, your role is this: to hold tightly the vision of restoring sacred relationship and to hold loosely the way it unfolds.

Guiding a wild church requires a wild leadership that is rooted in relationship with the living systems of a place. There are no gurus in nature. In any healthy ecosystem, there is no particular being in the forest who tells everyone else what to do. Rather, there are networks of interconnection. Nature is our teacher, our companion, our confidant, and our catalyst to tap into sacred wisdom. Leaders are needed not to tell people what to do or how to be ecologically spiritual. We are there to invite people to avail themselves of the Holy, in reverent awareness. The Holy Presence does the rest.

Justine Huxley, former director of St. Ethelburga's Centre, and Anna Kovasna of the Global Ecovillage Network lead a project called *Kincentric Leadership through the Polycrisis.* Described as "an experimental field that places direct collaboration with the more-than-human world at the heart of all interventions, strategy, culture and ways of working," kincentric leadership "asks that we include radically other ways of being, learn from multiple forms of intelligence, and that we use our influence to move towards a shared purpose of reciprocal respect, dignity and mutual thriving."

"But ask the animals what they think and let them teach you; let the birds speak to your heart. Put your ear to the earth— learn the basics. Listen ... the fish in the ocean will tell you their stories" (Job 12:7–12, *The Message*).

16

The kincentric model, which we strive to adopt in wild churches, is rooted in a deep sense of our belonging with all of life. It aims to "de-center humanity as neither more nor less important than bats, clouds, or rainforests." Leading a wild church with kinship values means you are more concerned with holding space for others to experience the Holy as they listen reverently to nature than directing others through your expertise and authoritative wisdom. What is needed most is your authenticity, vulnerability, and presence.

HOLDING THE CONTAINER

You can't create a formula for transformation. But you can hold space for it. Holding space simply means that you are focused on creating a safe, supportive, and respectful environment for others to share from their hearts, to ask questions, and to express themselves without feeling judged or corrected. You're inviting people into a vulnerable space where nobody is invisible, where each person is learning to trust their own experience with the Divine in the shape of a lily pad or composting leaves.

Leaders invite each participant to trust their own inner authority rather than acting as if the leader is the authority. This is a significant and essential break from long-held paradigms of religious leadership. We step aside so others can experience what they experience, access their own inner genius, and trust their particular relationship with the Divine. It is more about listening than being heard.

"There's a way that nature speaks, that land speaks.
Most of the time we are simply not patient enough,
quiet enough, to pay attention to the story."
—Linda Hogan

When a seed is planted in your soul to start a wild church, you'll know. You may find yourself longing for more time in nature, wandering slowly on the edges of wildish places near your home, wishing you had others to experience the reality of our mystical connection with all that is. Pay close attention to that

Can you get paid to lead a wild church? Most wild churches have a core group of fewer than twenty people, so financial support for the leaders in the traditional sense of passing a collection basket is unlikely. Some have been able to find support through partnerships with local environmental or religious organizations or by registering their wild churches as nonprofit organizations and applying for grants. A few have worked with their local religious communities or denominations to fund their community as an innovative form of church.

yearning. What that seed grows into will be particular to you, your vision and background, the ecosystem where you live, the people who are drawn to join you. Your wild church may wind up being very different than you expect!

A wild place may beckon you into conversation. Perhaps it will coax you to start a wild church under a particular tree, beside a particular bend of the creek, or in a circle in the middle of a city park. Your rational mind might start to question this beckoning. But spirituality—wild or tamed—is not centered in the mind. You'll feel it in your body, your intuition, when you allow a place to choose you.

There are no templates for wild spiritual leadership because the whole movement is built on relationship. And relationship is always particular. What one leader does in rural Idaho, alongside a group of local Mennonites who are farmers and horticulturalists, will differ from what another leader does in Southern California, with a group of burned-out corporate executives and youth climate activists. And so it is with place too. A wild church meeting outside in northern Ontario winters will be different from what a wild church looks like in a Texan summer.

HONORING DIVERSE SPIRITUALITIES

The container you hold as a wild church leader is a living system, an ecosystem in which each organism, human and more-than-human, has their own life and growth pattern. The carrot cannot tell the garlic to grow faster or deeper. As the leader, you honor the unique spiritual language and orientation of each person, trusting that their unfolding is happening in the way that is best for them. Listening deeply, leaders also notice interconnecting threads, paying attention when a group of hawks circles, when a great wind blows through, or when stories brought back from a time of wandering weave together in overlapping themes.

Like a healthy ecosystem rich in diversity, you are welcoming a range of spiritual traditions held by those in your group. You aren't trying to tell them to abandon their religion to enter into a new, wilder one. You are simply inviting all who are gathered to deepen into their own spirituality through an intimate connection with Earth. Essentially, you're holding space for sacred conversation: between one another and between each person and particular others who are not human. All of it is prayer.

EDGE-WALKING

We are edge-walkers. We walk along the edges between an old story of domination and exploitation and a new story, rooted in kindred interconnection, which has not yet fully emerged. This liminal space between stories is unboxed and full of unknowns as we experiment together with post-patriarchal leadership models and post-dogmatic spiritual practices.

Be gentle as you follow your heart. Listen to your own timing and to the synchronicities that might lead you. Feel into it and let it take root; let it become what it will. May the questions in the Field Notes section in the back of the book and the stories throughout the following chapters offer you inspiration to step into your own wild leadership.

Our best advice for getting started is this: *just start*. Find a place, set a date, tell some friends, and avail yourselves to the sacred wild. Honestly, it's that simple. Trust your heart's wild longing. As poet David Wagoner says, "Let the trees find you."

STORIES & PRACTICES

NAMING YOUR COMMUNITY. Many wild churches simply identify their gatherings with either Wild Church or Church of the Wild, along with the name of the bioregion, watershed, or state, country, city: Clearwater Church of the Wild or Wild Church of Edmonton or Wild Church Germany. Some avoid words like *church* or *wild* altogether. Here are a few of the names of wild churches within the network: Wild Earth Spiritual Community, Sacred Ground, Gathering Ground, Two Trees Talking, Wild Sacred, Church of the Woods, Burning Bush Forest Church, Chapel in the Pines, Wild Journey, Earth Church, Cathedral of the Wild, Flicker: a Pop-Up Wild Church, Sanctuary of the Wild, Church of the Wild River, Wind from the Sea, The Farm Sanctuary, Sacred Spirits of Maine, Transfiguration Preserve, Sisters of the Sacred Wild, Coffee Outside, The Omega Sanctuary, Wild Church of the Singing River, Mindful Outdoor Experience, Bamboo Encounter, Wild Belongings, Forest Edge Cearcall, Eternal Gardens, Divine Nature, Skywanda Sanctuary, Wild Church at Meadow View Farm, Sacred Journeys Community, groWING, Brave Circles, Wild Light Spiritual Oasis, Conservation Creek Sanctuary, Tahoma Wild, El Pueblito, Salal + Cedar, Wilderness Church, Anam Cara Earth Gatherings, Wild Friends Church, Woodland Worship, Nourish in Nature, Earth Monks: a new monastic community, Wild Spirit, Church of the Wild Blue Yonder, Sanctuary of the Wild, Outdoor Chaplain, Wild Church of the Watershed, Pine Pulpit, Holy Thresholds Wild Church, Holy Quest Nature Walks, Sacred Circles Wild Church, Wilderness Wanderers, Wild Journey, Earth Dream Nature Area, Sacred SoulScapes, Wild Communion, Wild

Grace Community, Wild Temples, WildWood Sundays, Church on the Prairie, Eco-Adoration, Cathedral of the Trees, Madonna of the Woods Wild Church, Church in Creation, The Milkweed, Roots of Life, The Furrow, Sacred Ground Community Church & Sangha, Fellowship of St. John Muir, Chemung River Wild Spirit, Sacred Earth, Temenos, Faith Among the Trees, Earthen Hands, North Star Community, Spirit of the Wild Earth Sanctuary, Wild Church Healing Pathways, Forest Temple—to name a few!

ASKING THE VULNERABLE QUESTIONS. Our ministry began by asking the question, "Where have all the young people gone from our churches—and why have they left?" The sincerity in asking led to a humbleness of heart, which led to a willingness to be vulnerable and uncomfortable. When I was approached about becoming the mission developer for this holy experiment, which has now become the wild church known as U.P. Wild, I also wanted to know the answer to these questions. Having seen about nine out of ten church friends no longer in church on Sundays, I have many friends now raising families yet having no spiritual connections with them.

So I met with over forty young adults at coffee shops and invited them to share their faith background, their struggles with the church, where they found connection in their lives, and what their values were. Long story short: most of the young adults I met with, who would be very unwilling to step back into a church, expressed a deep connection with nature. We live in the Upper Peninsula of Michigan, which has thousands of miles of wilderness, so this makes sense in our context. But as many can attest, this is not an uncommon sentiment. I think we all have this desire to be in nature, which is a part of us, "from dust you came and to dust you shall return."—*Lanni Lantto, U.P. Wild Church, Marquette, MI*

FROM INDOOR CHURCH TO WILD CHURCH. In the beautiful Hill Country of central Texas, one small "regular" church moved outdoors. New Life is a part of the Evangelical Lutheran Church in America (ELCA), the largest Lutheran body in the United States. New Life was, in 2013, a relatively new church in a ranching-community-turned-suburb. The small congregation had big dreams of a church building on ten acres of ranch land on the edge of town. But the focus shifted. People moved to this place, in large part, for its natural beauty. People were looking for ways to connect with God more deeply—new and also ancient ways of being close to God in creation. The congregation looked at the small piece of land they had grown to love, at the giant century-old live oak trees and the cedar that had overgrown goat pens, and they wondered if the land itself was the church, not the future building.

So they cleared barbed wire, learned about the native grasses, and gathered under the oaks, where a horse trough became an altar. They made a labyrinth and a walking trail with stations of the cross constructed from found metal and beautiful stones. Adults met under one tree for Bible study after church and children under another for Godly Play, a Montessori-based approach. Musicians used to outdoor venues contributed to a simple but recognizably Lutheran service. The land's wild grapes were harvested to make communion wine. Area Lutheran congregations chipped in to buy an event tent for rainy Sundays. They let go of the office-complex rental space and moved the liturgical furniture out to the land as part of the Maundy Thursday stripping of the altar. Wild Church

happened and grew as a new expression of one of the mainline
Protestant denominations.

And the land prayed with the people, and the birds sang along,
and the people were humbled and amazed by the seasons and the
small changes all year round in that one prayed-on, played-on,
worshiped-on holy space. And New Life continues.—*Carmen Retzlaff, founder and original pastor of New Life Lutheran Church: A Wild
Church, Dripping Springs, TX*

DISCERNING PLACE. We spent a long time looking for a place
that was accessible but not so accessible that there are a million
other people there. We knew we needed access to major highways
since all our folk come from a mix of Washington, DC; Maryland; and Virginia. We have settled on a space that has become
our home base, a space we know and honor deeply. It is part of
the C&O Canal Historical Park on the banks of the Potomac. We
found a spot off the beaten path that is still easy to find. But in
winter, when we need a fire to warm us, we meet once a month on
the grounds of Dayspring Retreat Center. Although it is a farther
drive for just about everyone, and we pay a small fee, the land
is soaked in silence and prayer.—*Sara Anders, Wild Earth Spiritual
Community, Washington, DC*

HOMESTEAD WILD CHURCH. We meet on our private homestead
in Vermont, which has meadows, ponds, forest, gardens, orchards,
vineyard, and lots of free-range chickens. This rural setting with
great diversity on the landscape is a privilege that we continual-
ly give thanks for as it provides endless gifts to our gatherings

throughout all seasons. —*Heather Wolfe, Taftsville Chapel's Wild Church at Meadow View Farm, Woodstock, VT*

REDEFINING WILD. Our site in a public park is not very wild as we meet between the river and a train track. The sound of the train becomes a challenge, as do the children's birthday parties often happening close by. But I feel we can find "wildness" in our hearts no matter where we are if that is our intention. —*Dana Jefferson, Allegheny Cathedral of the Wild, Huntingdon, PA*

ACCESSIBILITY AND THE WILD. We have met in three different spots so far. The property on the Laguna de Santa Rosa Foundation doesn't feel as wild as one of the regional parks, but it is accessible for people with disabilities and has great bathrooms. Even though it's not as wild, they do have a lovely native garden and beautiful views of the laguna. We have also met on the land that they steward, which is a bit more wild, as well as a county regional park. This is where it has felt most wild and free to wander. Yet because it is a regional park, we are required to get a special-use permit. It is a challenge to find all the things desired for an accessible, wild, and yet bathroom-friendly place, yet it has been working out beautifully. Part of the process is acknowledging the human experience and impact on wild places. —*Mindy Braun, Wild Journey, Santa Rosa, CA*

WILD CHURCH IN PUBLIC PARKS. Our regular meeting area is in the city in a public park and can be reached by car, public transit, or bicycle, which is important to us. It is a forested park with a good amount of biodiversity and hard-packed wood-chip trails. We meet along the banks of a creek and among trees that are over a century old, reflecting the kind of forest that would have covered much of this area before urbanization and agriculture took over. It feels relatively wild, though we hear the constant hum of traffic from a nearby freeway. This serves as a good reminder to us of our human impact on our more-than-human neighbors who live in that place. We have explored areas outside the city, but participants prefer to not have to drive that far.—*Wendy Janzen, Burning Bush Forest Church, Kitchener-Waterloo, ON*

FEELING WELCOMED TO A PLACE . . . OR NOT. We gather in a lime beech forest upon a hill and usually feel very welcomed there. One day I decided to go there on my own by night to get the full range of light, weather, and the special atmosphere connected to this very place. At midnight, I got on my mountain bike and reached our place within total darkness. I didn't expect this place to be so dark. What surprised me even more was the feeling of not feeling welcomed there. It was as if the place said, "You are and will be always welcomed here but not at night. When the sun leaves this place, we belong to the creatures of night and for resting and healing." So I took my bike and went home with the impression of having learned an important lesson.—*Arnd Corts, Wild Church Sauerland, Germany*

PARTNERSHIP WITH A LOCAL CHURCH OR ORGANIZATION. I approached a local Unitarian church and offered to lead a wild church once a month. They reciprocated by paying me and doing all the outreach, etc. It is an outlet for me but one that is being honored by the church by paying me for my efforts. I am a full-time artist, so this little monthly token of reciprocity is actually helpful to me.—*Mary Abma, Wild-Edge Offerings, Bright's Grove, ON*

PARTNERSHIP WITH RETREAT CENTERS AND PARKS. The United Church of Canada, where we are both ordained, held an outdoor worship service in the Algonquin Provincial Park in their Outdoor Theatre every summer since the 1950s. We heard this tradition was going to be lost when the park was restructured, so we made a proposal to the local region of the United Church that we would take over the leadership of this outdoor worship if it could be reimagined as a forest church. We were adamant that this was not an indoor service taken outdoors but a wild church service that took seriously the more-than-human world as co-participant, teacher, and preacher. Thus, Cathedral of the Trees–Algonquin Park was born.

We applied for and received funding for this. Our costs included the purchase of a "new to us" camper-trailer and of course park fees for using a campsite throughout the summer. And then we recruited local clergy who were interested in exploring wild church to lead the weekly service. In exchange, the clergy get to stay in Algonquin Park at the Lake of Two Rivers campground in the church-owned trailer. Leaders are not paid for their work, but the respite opportunity in this amazing natural setting means we have a long list of interested leaders each year.

We provide wild church leadership training for these clergy and a template of a forest church service for them as a jumping-off point. The park also does not schedule anything else in the

Outdoor Theatre on Sunday mornings and lists the forest church service in the park newspaper. It is now one of the services they provide to the thousands of campers who use its many campgrounds each summer.—*Marilyn Zehr and Svinda Heinrichs, Cathedral of the Trees, Maynooth, ON*

PARTNERSHIP WITH DENOMINATIONS. I was able to pay myself a salary by raising funds from two regional denominational institutions who were looking to fund new innovative ministries: the Episcopal Diocese of Northern Michigan and the ELCA's Northern Great Lakes Synod. I was hired as the mission developer for this joint initiative, and I applied for many different grants. The denominations, then, offered matching funds. I need to reapply every year, and so I've started to ask people in my growing community to support our wild church as well.

There are many positives in having such collaborative support. But it comes with the hierarchical bureaucracy of multiple superiors (bishops, canons, committees), who all have an opinion. There are many rules to follow that may not align with your wild church's values. You always need to ask yourself, "Is this worth the financial assistance?"—*Lanni Lantto, U.P. Wild, Upper Peninsula, MI*

UNAPOLOGETICALLY SHARING YOUR TRADITION. Most of our members identify as Christian, and many have a Sunday morning community where they worship. Others are more at the edges of church. We have had folks join us who are Buddhist, Muslim, Jewish, pagan, Indigenous spiritual practitioners, agnostics, and atheists. We are clear and unapologetic about our Christian identity and practice. And we don't ask anyone to participate in ways that feel uncomfortable to them. We always offer the opportunity to "pass," and we try to emphasize, in whatever we do, that everyone is invited and no one is required.—*Laurel Dykstra, Salal + Cedar, Vancouver, BC*

HOLDING DIVERSE SPIRITUAL TRADITIONS. Most of the participants have had a Christian upbringing revolving around traditional church services and are looking for something deeper and more expansive. They have all brought a potent desire to experience the natural world more intimately. There have been some participants who practice Buddhism and some who are very aligned with Celtic spirituality. My approach is cross-cultural but not liturgical. I do not have a relationship with the Bible so tend not to quote from it, and while my leaning is toward Native American and Indigenous traditions, I do offer quotes, songs, and stories from a variety of spiritual traditions. A deep respect for Earth and nature prevails.— *Tamara Grenier, Lowcountry Wild Church, Charleston / Johns Island, SC*

NAMING YOUR SPIRITUAL LENS. When I introduce myself, I share my spiritual lens, which is situated on the edge of Christianity within an animate Celtic cosmology. It's important to name my approach and to let the group know that their religious background, tradition, or lack of tradition is welcome. It seems that my spiritual orientation continues to evolve, so I also hold my lens loosely. People who attend range from those who are still involved in traditional church, retired priests, those who have left and are deconstructing their Christian heritage, pagan, Buddhist, and spiritual but not religious. I want people to know that we aren't trying to change anybody's beliefs but that wild church can be a place of healing spiritual wounds and a practice of rewilding our spirituality, whatever that may be.—*Valerie Luna Serrels*

EVOLVING SPIRITUAL TRADITIONS. We identify ourselves through a "melding of traditions." Since 2009, our church/sangha has been a confluence of the beneficial teachings of Buddhism, Christianity, and Earth-centered spirituality. Having discovered Victoria Loorz's book *Church of the Wild*, Sacred Ground now offers Church of the Wild / Sangha of All Beings services each month. Given our focus, for each Sacred Ground Church of the Wild service, we have at least one reading from the Judeo-Christian Bible and one reading from the writings of the late Vietnamese Zen Buddhist monk, Thich Nhat Hanh, whose writings and mindfulness trainings serve as a foundational grounding for our spiritual community.—*Michael Malley, Sacred Ground Community Church & Sangha, Columbus, OH*

INTENTIONALLY INTERFAITH AND LEARNING. Our group is specifically interfaith. Our members range from Ba'Hai, Native American, Gnostic, pagan, Christian, and Jewish to nature lovers without a specific spiritual or religious affiliation. This is managed by careful use of language in our services as well as inviting those present to internally substitute any terms that make them uncomfortable. All those attending have been open-minded and appear to appreciate learning from each other.—*Dana Jefferson, Allegheny Cathedral of the Wild, Huntingdon, PA*

WIDENING THE COMMUNITY. Each of our gatherings is so sweet, but my favorite ones are when our friends who are unhoused participate in Forest Church. Nothing is better than the sense of looking around the circle and seeing people who are unhoused next to suburban moms next to little kids next to burned-out pastors next to atheists next to lawyers next to teenagers next to single grandmas next to LGBTQ+ friends next to power hikers next to senior citizens. It is one of the prettiest things in the world: all together, seeking healing and community on the land.—*Kathy Escobar, Forest Church Golden, CO*

A MINISTRY FOR THE MINISTERS. Though predominantly Mennonite, our gathering includes people from a variety of Christ-centered faiths. I imagined the gathering attracting people outside of organized religion, but that hasn't happened yet for us. What has happened, and was unexpected, is how many pastors are in attendance! I would not have guessed this would be such a ministry to those who minister, but it makes sense. This can be their church, a place to come and fill their spiritual bucket.—*Heather Wolfe, Wild Church Taftsville Chapel, Woodstock, VT*

ECLECTIC AND DECONSTRUCTING. Forest Church is a very spiritually eclectic group, with most originally coming from the

Christian tradition in some way, having experienced a faith deconstruction, and ended up far more open to wider and inclusive spiritual practices. We have had to be very careful about triggering language and work hard at making all our liturgies a mix of spiritual traditions, readings, poems, and experiences. That has made it so much more accessible to everyone.

Because *church* is in our name, it has made some people who are extra allergic to church wary, and we have had to explain to them that it's not overtly Christian but spiritual and soulful and inclusive for all spiritual expressions. Once they taste it, they get it. We've wrestled with whether or not to keep *church* in the name, but we are committed to playing our part in redeeming some of those past experiences. We want to provide a healing space for what "church" can be, especially for people who have found themselves on the outside of everything they had once known.
—*Kathy Escobar, Forest Church, Golden, CO*

STRUGGLES AND SUPPORT. I felt the ache of loneliness in leading a Wild Church by myself before our winter gathering. Daylight Savings was fast approaching, and the cold, gray mornings began to send a panic through me. I spun into a whirl of questioning about whether we should move our gathering indoors, and so I called different facilities, gathering information about costs. Eventually, I had to make the decision that the cost was too great for such a small community. I felt alone in making this decision as my coleader was absent due to a hard personal loss. I struggled with the feeling I had often felt in traditional ministry: of all the details and their subsequent execution landing on my shoulders. I felt solely responsible for making our little gathering happen and the fear that if I didn't, our Wild Church would no longer exist.

This loneliness began to dissolve as I made the bold choice to simply talk about it. I posted a message on The Ecosystem (an online platform that hosts Wild Church Network leaders), and I was surprised by the many empathic and encouraging responses I received. People I hadn't even met yet chimed in with their thoughts, and the loneliness I had felt began to fade. Furthermore, my panic about gathering over winter began to subside as I remembered one of our members sharing about how much he appreciated us still meeting, even in the rain, because it reminded him that life still continues in the winter. Through this experience, I was able to accept that loneliness may be a part of leading a Wild Church solo—but so is the radical and ever-present community of all living things. — *Colette Eaton, Wild Church Portland, Portland, OR*

WHEN WORDS DON'T FIT. We began in April 2018 as Church of the Wild, Metro MD, DC, VA. We have participants from several different spiritual traditions, including nones and dones, Jain, Jewish, pagan, and Christian. Over time, it became clear that the term *church* was not welcoming to those who don't identify as Christian. So we changed our name to Wild Earth Spiritual Community. The name change has indeed brought a wider variety of seekers. But it wasn't an easy transition.

While we've practiced honoring and respecting the path of each person present, we had a challenging experience when two of our attendees clashed over the term *Goddess*, which was the term one participant used for the Divine. Another protested, and since we were still a new community, a fragile group, this rift threatened our connection to one another. We called in a trained facilitator to mediate the tensions between the two, but one decided to leave our group.

This incident made it clear that it behooved us to state clearly what we expect from every participant. At most of our gatherings now, we state in our mission, "We encourage one another's spiritual path and attentively nurture our own while challenging each other to live and act responsibly on behalf of Earth."

To explore the Great Mystery free of dogma and hierarchy, and in accordance with our desire to authentically welcome all, we intentionally choose not to be affiliated with any one denomination or spiritual tradition. We listen to and learn from each of our stories, including the stories of Earth (such as tree, soil, and water). We approach our gatherings from an interspiritual perspective. We honor the common thread of oneness with Earth's divine mystery found in most ancient religions and spiritual practices.—*Sarah Anders, Wild Earth Spiritual Community, Washington, DC*

3
ARRIVAL
Grounding in Sacred Presence

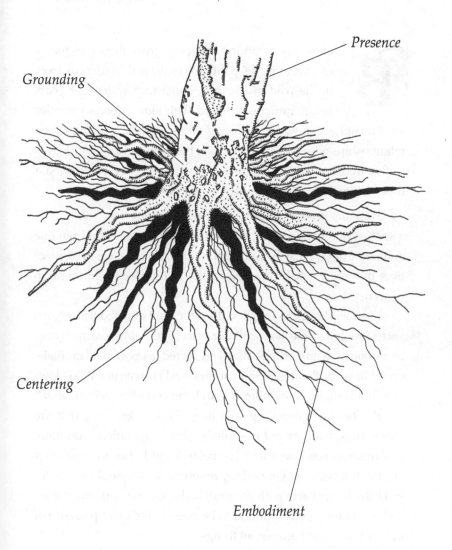

Presence

Grounding

Centering

Embodiment

"The natural world—that world where we already belong—is an alluring invitation into the sacred, into relationship with something larger. And that very sacred presence invites us into the wild. The whole process is holy. It is a dynamic, a reciprocity, a loving conversation, a relationship—one that includes me and you and God and the whole wild, alive world."

—*Church of the Wild*

efore any grounded being can grow, their seed focuses on rooting deep into the moist soil. Young oak trees in the wild invest in a robust root system for years before growing upward. This slow process provides a solid connection with the ground while establishing supportive relationships with the other beings in their new world. Within two to five decades, when oak trees mature, they have established a root system three times the size of their crown.

Humans need to be more intentional about their rooting. As a species caught in a dominant culture of disconnection from one another, from the Earth, and from our own bodies, we need practices that root us back into the reality of our deep connection to the ecosystem.

Most wild churches begin with some kind of embodied experience of rooted connection with our place. Grounding practices help us reconnect with Earth as alive and sacred; as poet William Blake says, "To see a World in a Grain of Sand and Heaven in a Wild Flower, to hold infinity in the palm of your hand and Eternity in an hour."

Practices of grounding stimulate ways of knowing that are rooted in our bodies, not our minds. Our imaginations, intuition, and inner senses that may have been discarded or undeveloped are invited back in. Grounding involves soul-to-soul or sole-to-soil listening to Earth with your full body, sensing with your heart, and awakening your intuition to be open to the quiet presence of the sacred in and between all things.

GROUNDING AS INTERCONNECTION

A wild church experience that begins with a grounding practice slows down and softens our bodies and eyes to allow us to interact with nature from our hearts. John O'Donohue wisely states, "When we walk on the earth with reverence, beauty will decide to trust us. The rushed heart and arrogant mind lack the gentleness and patience to enter that embrace." The trees and animals and other beings are already fully present and grounded; they wait for us to join them.

> Some creation-focused hymns in indoor churches offer an invitation to the creation to *join us* in worship. Wild church moves beyond this human-centric orientation: the trees and beetles and creeks are in a perpetual state of worship, and they are inviting *us* in. But we can only hear the beckoning if our hearts are open.

Sometimes removing your shoes and connecting your bare feet with the Earth helps to sync with her natural rhythms and plentiful electrons. Our bodies and psyches ache for this intimate reconnection, especially when we've denied our skin this sensual contact for a long time. Of course, we don't need to rely on bare feet. Simply standing in the place where we are and taking a moment to notice the ground beneath our feet can ground us back into our essential relatedness with the other beings in our place.

Grounding into place and time involves attuning our bodies to the body of the Earth in the particular ecosystem where we are, noticing how our bodies feel, and opening our five senses to engage the more-than-human world. It's also about attuning to particular seasonal energies and offering our full presence to this place, this time. Winter has a different feel than spring. Full moons affect us in different ways than new moons. Noticing how these seasonal shifts feel for us is a grounding into the wisdom of these fluctuations.

Grounding into the invisible dimension of any location is important as well. The spiritual presence that connects our bodies with the tree growing on the bank of the river, or your mother on the other side of the country, is real. Grounding practices like those offered in this chapter can help awaken participants to that which can't be seen with our eyes or heard with our ears but is just as alive as the material world. Physicists, mystics, and Indigenous wisdom-keepers know that the material world itself is more like condensed energy and light. We can't actually see our roots, but we can feel when we are rooted. We can't experience infinity, but when we are fully absorbed in a creative flow or in a state of awe, it seems as if time stands still. Our inner sensing practices help wild church participants to tune in to the conversation going on around us all the time.

OPENING TO PRESENCE

When our minds settle down and our hearts open, we can more easily connect with divine presence within us and around us. Although our inner sensing system has been systematically shut down over the centuries by a modern world focused on linear thinking and analysis, we still can access it. This inner sensing includes intuition and instinct, heart and body awareness. Accessing this dormant part of ourselves might feel unfamiliar or

Without diminishing how important the logistics are for a gathering—communicating well with those who are coming, having everything you need—the most important quality of a good gathering hinges on how present you are to the place where you are, the people who come, and yourself.

uncomfortable since it goes against the modern cultural story of a de-enchanted world devoid of spiritual reality.

Your own grounding practices can often be easily adapted to a wild church gathering. Do you practice yoga? Breathwork? Contemplative prayer? Honor your own spiritual traditions and practices and bring them in. The following stories and practices from various wild church leaders offer different approaches to grounding and centering, including holding silence, drumming, performing guided meditation, chanting, noticing the breath, and practicing slow movements. All can initiate a shift of focus from the mind to the heart, from the externalized to the embodied.

STORIES & PRACTICES

ARRIVING AND ATTUNING AS SPIRITUAL PRACTICE. Wild church really begins when the fir, red spruce, and birch trees greet my husband and me on the final mile of the road leading to our meeting spot in the George Washington National Forest. When we roll down the windows to hear if the creek is trickling or rushing, we can feel that inner shift begin. The sounds of the water, the smell of pine, and the play of light and shadow tell us what time of year it is. As we downshift the car, we shift into slow time. It takes an intentional slowing down to arrive. And not like the getting-to-the-place, parking-the-car, and walking-in kind of arrival. I mean to fully arrive with all of who I am: to attune to the trees and ground and senses, attune to soul within and to the invisible surround.

Once the others come, I invite them to slow down, too, to breathe, to pause the running mind scripts and activities. Beginning with a time of silence and deep breathing, we take a few minutes to open to our five senses, integrating even the traffic and barking dogs. We open our hearing to the rushing water or wind, the bird song; our taste to pine or smoke; and our touch to the ground around us.

I then lead a short guided meditation into the alive landscape within us, closing our eyes and shifting from our five senses to our inner spiritual senses, down into our intuitive heart center and our soulscape, in relationship with the physicality and energy of the place.—*Valerie Luna Serrels*

SILENT WORTH-SHIP. *Here is a grounding meditation that can open a wild church service. Substitute references to your place and context.*

Let us begin with a time of silence. It's not really silence, though, because the land is alive with sound. It's more like inviting our own inner silence. We are here to listen in on a holy conversation already going on in this prairie, on this spring day. As in any conversation, silence is necessary to listen to the voices of the others with all our senses. [*Spend five minutes (or more) in silence. Then offer a prayer/meditation:*]

Listen to your breath. Listen to the wind. We are connected through the breath of God. Slowly allow yourself to relax into this welcoming place. You belong here with these particular trees and this soil, held together by a web of miraculous mycelium, these flowers who show up in the spring and the stones and the flies and scrub jays and poison ivy. Listen for the water, arteries of life flowing throughout the planet mirroring the arteries of blood flowing through your own body. You are a welcome part of this ecosystem. They welcome us because they have not forgotten that we are related, that we come from the same dust and return to the same dust. Take another deep breath of gratitude to acknowledge that our lives are fully dependent on the healthy functioning of this particular biosystem.

We are here as an expression of worship, which means "declaring the worth of." We are here as an act of religion, *religios.* Like ligaments that hold the bones of the world together, religion simply means reconnection. We are here to restore a loving and kindred relationship with the rest of the natural world, as a spiritual practice.—*Victoria Loorz*

EIGHT DIRECTIONS PRAYER. *Directional prayers are practiced by many cultures. They are a spiritual practice that orients us to our place*

and connects us with the miraculous whole, reminding us that we belong to this land, not the other way around. Different cultures and individuals attribute different meanings to each direction. There is no getting it right. There is no doing it wrong.

EAST: [*Make an embodied gesture of sending.*] Let's stand and face toward the East with an embodied gesture of sending blessings to all who are east of us. Imagine the mountains and cities, the humans and more-than-humans while you send your blessings. In particular, we send blessings and love to all who are suffering and in need of fresh hope and new life. [*Make a gesture of receiving.*] And now create a movement of receiving blessings from the beings in the East, with gratitude.

The East often represents the element of *Air*, which is associated with the morning, springtime, and beginnings of new life. The rising sun. With deep gratitude, imagine your breath connecting you to the trees who create oxygen. Imagine the breathing together of all things. One of Mary Oliver's poems asks, "Are you breathing just a little and calling it a life?" Hold that question and ask yourself: what new life is longing to be expressed through me now, at this point in my life, at this moment in history, in this place, with these people? [*Pause.*] Hold that question.

Take a deep breath and exhale as you bow in honor to the Spirit, the Ruach, the Wind, the element of Air we all depend on for life. Selah.

SOUTH: [*Repeat the gestures of sending and receiving of blessings.*] Face the South, which is associated in many cultures with the element of *Fire*: we think of the noonday sun and summer. The South invites us to open up all of our senses and feel into our embodiment as creatures of the Earth. Notice the beings and elements and people close to you. Take in the trees and flowers and colors, and open your ears to listen to every sound, and even the sounds beneath the sounds. Feel within you into the fiery passions calling you to wake up and listen, perhaps to follow a new path that broadens your vision to those who need your attention, your medicine, your unique gift to heal the world.

Bow toward the South and all who dwell there, toward the fire within you and within all things, toward Mystery who connects and enflames all things. Selah.

WEST: [*Begin again with sending and receiving blessings.*] The West is sometimes associated with the element of *Water*: this evokes twilight or the autumnal season. Imagine the waters to the West. Water yields, reminding us to surrender to what must end and die, to what has served its purpose in your life and is ready to be let go. West is where the sun sets, inviting us to surrender those things in life that no longer serve us or the world, to make room for what is longing to be made new.

Bow to the Mystery of the West with a willingness to allow the sacred silence to dance within you. Selah.

NORTH: [*Sending and receiving blessings.*] Turn to the North, which is often associated with the dark, with winter, and with the elements of Earth. We think of the rocks, mountains, trees, creatures. The solid way they are who they are. With gratitude and open arms, with an emptiness that acknowledges that we are a gift not by what we own or what we do but simply and deeply and honestly by being who we are. Feel that. [*Pause.*] As you become more and more fully who you truly already are, you recognize that you are called to be engaged not just with your own small life and concerns but to be engaged with the repair of the world.

Bow toward the North to acknowledge that you belong to this Earth and are called to be partners with all who dwell here, in the great healing and transformation happening in the world now. Selah.

ABOVE: [*Sending and receiving blessings.*] Look up, reach up toward the mystery of the universe, the stars we can't see right now

because of the miracle of the sun. Look up into an awareness that life is more than what we see before us. Imagine the miracle of our atmosphere, regulating heat and climate. Recognize the limitless miracle of planets and universes and galaxies engaged in a cosmic conversation, keeping all things working together.

Looking up, we remember that we belong to a story and a system of life much larger than the worries and concerns that consume us every day. With gratitude, we bow. Selah.

BELOW: [*Sending and receiving blessings.*] Look down now and touch the ground if you can. Imagine the roots of these trees interconnecting with all the other alive beings in the soil. Imagine the bugs and mycelium that keep the region healthy, transporting nutrients and transmuting death from one creature into life for another. There is a conversation going on beneath our feet all the time, connecting all things. Even us. Imagine below the soil, the waters flowing deep down beneath us and beneath that, the core of fire that animates all that is alive.

We are grateful for all our ancestors who came before us and for the ancestors of this land, whose spirits remain with us and whose physical bodies are now part, again, of the Earth that sustains us. Selah.

WITHIN: [*Sending and receiving blessings.*] Now, face within you. With gratitude for the living systems inside you that keep you alive. Imagine your nervous system, bones, organs, blood, air. Turn inward to your sacred center, where your DNA has knit together a unique and important human who belongs here, who is important here, who is needed here. Listen to that conversation within you. Not the one that chatters with to-do lists and self-criticism but the deeper conversation, the one that requires quiet and calm listening. This conversation is what some call Christ within you. The recognition of Namaste. The sacred in you and in each other and within all things. Selah.

BETWEEN: [*Sending and receiving blessings.*] And finally, the eighth direction: between. Bow to one another, to the reality that Christ is alive in all of us, in all things. That our connection between one another is a web of aliveness, a sacred reciprocity, a conversation holding us all together. Amen. — *Victoria Loorz*

DRUMMING AS GROUNDING. Drumming is an important ritual that syncs our heartbeats, increases our vibrational connection, and encourages transition into the body from our usual occupancy in the head. Without speaking, and as the Spirit leads us, we drum before we "formally" begin. Sometimes people are animatedly talking or greeting one another while others are drumming, sometimes it is too cold or hot to drum, sometimes it becomes playful and fun, and sometimes it is uniquely and richly contemplative. Usually there is a period of silence following the drumming to listen to the place herself.—*Sarah Anders, Wild Earth Spiritual Community, Washington, DC*

CHANTING. We are lucky to have several gifted song keepers in our group. But even if you don't have people who can lead singing, a simple chant serves to ground and connect the group. We chant a capella "What We Need Is Here," composed by Amy McCreath, several times at the beginning of just about every gathering.— *Sarah Anders, Wild Earth Spiritual Community, Washington, DC*

BREATH OF GROUNDING. *As we begin our gatherings, we seek to ground ourselves for many reasons. Primarily it is to allow us to become*

fully present to the land, to the more-than-humans who call this particular sacred space home, and to those who share our circle with us. We say something like this:

We invite you to close your eyes or to soften your focus. Do what is necessary to be comfortable in your space. Allow your body to become still. Take a deep breath.

Breathe! Breathe the sky. Breathe the gift of life offered by the plants and trees. Breathe in fully that relationship of reciprocity—that miracle that allows our exhalations to offer life to others and that allows their exhalations to bring the gift of life to us. Breathe and let your body relax into this space and this place.

When you exhale, release all that keeps you from being fully present in this moment.

As you breathe in, breathe in the presence of holiness. The holiness that surrounds us, the holiness that sits beside us, the holiness that lives within us.

Open yourself, open your senses, open your heart to this space. Listen, feel the air on your face, smell the scent of spring/summer/fall/winter, and taste the gift of life!

When you feel fully present to this moment—and to this place and the life she holds—open your eyes and see yourself in a circle of life that is vaster than we can imagine.—*LeAnn Blackert, Wild Church BC, BC*

BOWING PRACTICE. *At our gatherings, we often practice returning to the Earth with a bow. We can do this standing, on the ground, or sitting.*

Start with sitting: Hands at my sides, I feel myself here, human, being, connecting Earth and sky.

Hands reach out and up to the sky, draw sky down into my earthly body, mix the light and dark, the active and still, the blossoming and the release of this form.

And then bow downward, bodysoul (body-heart-mind-soul) returning to the Earth with reverence and humility, returning. Ashes to ashes, dust to dust, growing from the Earth, returning to the Earth. Head bowed, lower than the heart, touching the Earth, hands open to receive. Surrendering this moment through the physicality of the bow. My body embodies it so that my heart and mind can learn this gesture as well.

Return, following the same pathway, hands to heart. Bringing the humble, solid, ever-supportive, and accepting presence of Earth up into my humanness, connecting sky and Earth. Take a moment to check in with yourself now. Sense inside your body. Feel your heart (hand over heart). Notice your mind.—*Katy Taylor, Wild Church Port Townsend, Port Townsend, WA*

AWAKENING YOUR SENSES. Grounding is an important part of our "wild" time: waking ourselves to be fully present to all that awaits us. Allow yourself to settle, to let your body rest.

Breathe the air. Breathe the sky! Inhale and exhale deeply, allowing yourself to find a natural rhythm, allowing yourself to slow down—body, mind, and spirit! Then slowly open your senses to this space.

Touch. Let your skin feel the air, the breeze, the warmth of the sun.

Hear. Pay attention to the sounds around you: birds calling in the fervor of springtime, squirrels chattering, ducks laughing, the trees "shussing" a whisper of acknowledgment that you are seen. Even the human sounds of cars and lawnmowers and people talking are part of this aliveness.

See. Let your eyes open to the specifics of your space—see what is around you, see your more-than-human neighbors welcoming you to their home.

Taste the deliciousness of life in this moment.

When you feel stilled all the way to your soul, breathe again. Open yourself to experiencing a deeper connection with holiness!—*Sarah Anders, Wild Earth Spiritual Community, Washington, DC*

4
ANCESTRAL REVERENCE
Acknowledging the Land's Story

Acknowledgment

Indigenous Stories

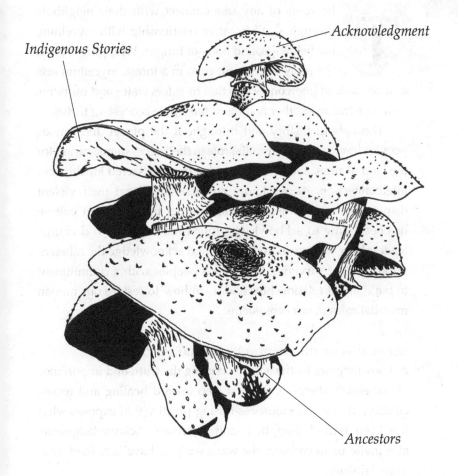

Ancestors

"The mountains, bushes, soil, insects, and ancestors are all acknowledged, honored, and included as co-congregants. And naming and acknowledging our watershed with gratitude helps us remember that we are utterly dependent on the gift of living water."

—*Church of the Wild*

he roots of any tree connect with their neighbors through a collaborative relationship with mycelium, the below-ground body of fungus. Wrapping around the roots of different trees in a forest, mycelium acts as a network of interconnection that transfers water and nutrients from one tree to another and helps the whole ecosystem thrive.

Throughout history and throughout the planet, Indigenous peoples have played a mycelial role in their ecosystems: caring for the land, waters, and creatures with a sense of sacred kinship and interconnection. As we know, colonization forced their violent displacement and erasure, a tragedy that the dominant culture has been slow to acknowledge, much less amend. Wild church leaders bear witness to this history and acknowledge the inherent importance of surviving Indigenous peoples with a commitment to build allied relationships and learn how to restore our human mycelial roles in our ecosystems.

ACKNOWLEDGE THE INDIGENOUS CARETAKERS OF PLACE

Acknowledgment—the act of accepting the truth and importance of someone's story—is the first step toward healing and recon- ciliation. It is a consciousness-raising practice that exposes what has been buried, forgotten, and rewritten. Acknowledgments also invite us to consider the ways we may have benefited from a cruel history.

It begins with research beyond a quick internet search. Who were the original peoples of the land where you are living?

Which Indigenous peoples now live there or nearby? What are the particular stories of colonization, resistance, removal, and survival etched into the fabric of your place? "Learning from and with indigenous dialogue partners—like any truly transforming encounter—is not first a matter of books and study but a long-term, in-person, first-person process," writes eco-theologian and professor Lisa Dahill. It's about developing relationships and taking steps to invest in acts of kindness and reconciliation.

Appropriation is a risk in this work. Conversation and relationship are the answer. If you are unsure about a practice you're considering adopting for your wild church, ask the people who are native to your place what they think and feel. Trust their guidance.

ACKNOWLEDGE THE LAND'S STORY

A land acknowledgment also acknowledges the story of the land, waters, and creatures of the place where you live and gather. The soil holds the crises and resiliencies in her memory. Acknowledging the ways that this land has survived, adapted, and continues to transform is a way to bear witness to the layers of natural changes through wildfires, floods, and earthquakes as well as human-made climate crises; animal migration paths disrupted by private property fences and roads; systematic destruction of the waters, rivers, soil; and rapid extinction of so many animals and plants.

Potawatomi botanist and author Robin Wall Kimmerer writes that her people have been violently severed from their ancestral lands and yet retain their deep spiritual connection with place. "The land shows bruises of an abusive relationship. It's not just the land that is broken, but more importantly our relationship to land," Kimmerer writes in *Braiding Sweetgrass*. "We cannot heal without hearing the stories of the land." The land remembers. Land acknowledgments are calls for us to remember too.

WELCOME DISCOMFORT

When you offer a land acknowledgment as part of your wild church gathering, be aware of the tendency to dilute the emotional impact of acknowledgments as they become more commonplace. Like all rituals, they can easily become rote and thin.

Chelsea Vowel, a Métis writer and lawyer from the Plains Cree people in Alberta, talks about land acknowledgments as tools of disruption. She exhorts, "If we think of territorial acknowledgments as sites of potential disruption, they can be transformative acts that to some extent undo Indigenous erasure." This disruption can cause an emotional reaction strong enough to dislodge a comfortable and dominant worldview of separation and superiority. Discomfort is a necessary emotion in transformation. There will be discomfort about our collective complicity in this history. You may fear you're not saying it right or doing everything you could and should be doing. There are no easy fixes for the violence of our past. But coming to terms with our own ancestral and spiritual lineages in ways that allow us to stay in the discomfort, engaging the land as sacred with gratitude, and reaching out to local Indigenous communities in ways that feel authentic and honoring can be a beginning.

If you're able, spend some time talking to relatives or research genealogy databases to find out your own ancestral lineages and lands. Reconnecting with your own ancestral Earth-based traditions can help shape how you approach practices and rituals.

Reverencing the land and the ancestors of the land with gratitude is an integral part of a wild church practice. Listening and responding with love to what else we may be called to do is a move from acknowledgment toward reconciliation.

STORIES & PRACTICES

CENTRAL OHIO LAND ACKNOWLEDGMENT AND ASPIRATION. We aspire to be here: in presence, with mindfulness, with awareness of the holiness of this space and all that is this place. We aspire toward gratitude, generosity, humility, and wonder.

We know that Shawnee people have dwelt here, as have other Indigenous peoples, and that they are present here right now, both twenty-first-century living descendants and spirits of the past. We know that moundbuilder peoples—the Fort Ancients, the Hopewell, and others—were here / are here / will always be here. We know that children laughed and played here thousands of years ago, hundreds of years ago, and in the mid-1800s, the 1930s, and last week. We know that much harm has come here: the destruction of the dense forests; the extinction and near-extinction of so many animal species; the exploitive and consummative growth of mills, factories, and shopping plazas; the concrete; the bloodshed; the tears.

You, Mother Earth, invite us to see it all. You, Mother Earth, ask us to move toward what is beneficial and healing. You, Mother Earth, ask us to re-member: for we are all spirit, we are all Earth, we are of the land, we are each of G-d.

We, the human beings, look to you, thirty-year-old black walnut, and to you, forty-year-old maple, and we ask, "Did your parents live here also?" We see you, ants, bees, birds, and we inquire, "For how many generations has your family lived in these parts?" We are aware of you, stone, and you, shell, and to you, we ask, "Were you carried here by ice-age glaciers? How did you arrive at this wondrous place?"

And we acknowledge you—blueness of sky, soft billow of cloud, hum of interstate traffic, faint roar of overhead jet—and we ask you, "Please tell us, how do we all live here in honor to our holy Mother Earth, in union with the Great Mystery beyond all names, and in respect of our teachers, the Buddha and the Christ, who have taught us that we are not separate from each other— that we are not separate from the land, the fire, the air, the water, and all our fellow earthly inhabitants?"

We, the human beings, acknowledge and accept our questions, our fears, our hopes, our not-knowing that we bring to this place, at this time, as members of this sacred beloved community of all beings. We are here—curious, grateful, alive, awake to worthy possibility. We are here with a commitment to being beings— wanting to stretch, learn, and grow; aspiring to live in deep relationship with our wider family of brothers and sisters, the Greater Earthen Family of animals, plants, and minerals, for the benefit of all.

We are here in gratitude. We thank you all. Amen and amen, and peace and amen.—*Michael Malley, Sacred Ground Church of the Wild & Sangha, Columbus, OH*

SHENANDOAH VALLEY LAND ACKNOWLEDGMENT. *We don't say this verbatim every time. It can become rote that way. But we share a version of this each time we meet. Someone reads the acknowledgment while I walk around behind our circle offering a gift—such as sunflower seeds, flower petals, pieces of apple, native wildflower seeds, water—to the Earth and the ancestors.*

We arrive fully here, on this land and its story, with all of our own stories and our ancestors' stories. Take a breath and feel yourself connected to this land as people of the Earth. This place that we love is the territory of the Monacan Nation, along with many other Indigenous peoples who traveled, hunted, and traded through these lands: the Siouan, Algonquian, and Haudenosaunee communities. We offer our respect and gratitude for their legacy of kinship with this place with this gift of [*name the gift*].

We lament the violent colonization of this land and the displacement of Indigenous peoples and creatures, and perhaps our own ancestral complicity. We acknowledge and name the trauma and suffering of African peoples who were brought here against their will and enslaved for profit. We lament the trauma and destruction of life from the Civil War fought here on these lands, and the continuation of racial injustice. We seek to heal broken relationship and the false separation of ourselves from this Earth and present ourselves here with love to the living descendants and ancient ancestors of this land and the land herself.—*Valerie Luna Serrels*

VENTURA RIVER WATERSHED ACKNOWLEDGMENT. We honor, in particular, the ancestral human caretakers of this land. This is a practice common to nearly all wild churches. The tree where we are sitting now was once a gathering place for the Indigenous Chumash peoples, who have lived in kindred relationship with this land for at least ten thousand years. Chumash elder Julie Tumamait-Stenslie tells us that this tree is where her grandmother once played, near her home along the river. She, along with her father and great-grandmother and great-great-grandmother for many more than seven generations, lived in an active, sacred relationship on this land. The Franciscan mission in nearby Ventura nearly wiped out her people in an effort to control them and use them as laborers. The Chumash culture and their way of life never recovered. It is important for us to specifically and intentionally remember and honor their ancestral and current presence, reckon with their tragic story, and invest in ways we can love more deeply in relationship with them.—*Victoria Loorz*

VERMONT LAND ACKNOWLEDGMENT. We greet each other and creation around us as kin, as sacred. We greet each other on the unceded ancestral homeland (n'dakinna) of the Western Abenaki past and present here within the Ottauquechee ("swift mountain stream") watershed. We acknowledge and honor with gratitude those who steward this place now and throughout the many generations, and we give great thanks to the Creator.—*Heather Wolfe, Wild Church Taftsville Chapel, Woodstock, VT*

VANCOUVER BRITISH COLUMBIA LAND ACKNOWLEDGMENT. *At Salal + Cedar, we begin every gathering by acknowledging that we are on Indigenous land. Various Indigenous people have told us words that come from the heart are better than words written on paper. So we don't have a written formula, but we take turns speaking what we have learned and stating our intentions. We also have a concrete financial part of our land acknowledgment, which is a formal commitment to pay a voluntary land tax each year to the people on whose lands we meet. There is a trust in development locally (Reciprocity Trust), but until they are ready, we are paying to Tsleil Waututh Sacred Trust. Here is an example of how I would start a service; other community members would do it differently or might add to mine.*

We start this time of prayer on the land by acknowledging that most of us in this circle are on this land as interlopers, squatters, or uninvited guests. These are lands and waters that care for and have cared for Musqueam, Squamish, Tsleil Waututh, Kwikwetlem, and Katzie people in reciprocal relationship from time immemorial. We acknowledge that we have a role in and benefit from the displacement of Indigenous people from their lands and that this puts us in a relationship of debt and obligation. We commit to seeking ways to live more justly in that relationship.—*Laurel Dykstra, Salal + Cedar, Vancouver, BC*

KELOWNA BRITISH COLUMBIA LAND ACKNOWLEDGMENT. *Speaking a land acknowledgment at the beginning of our gatherings is a first step in living into true reconciliation with local Indigenous peoples. It is also an important reminder that we are all called to live in right relationship with the lands which we call home. Indigenous communities remind us that land is more than a geographical location. The land is a place of deep spiritual connection with Great Mystery.*

We acknowledge that our gatherings take place on the unceded ancestral lands of the Syilx/Okanagan and Secwepemc Nations. We also recognize and name the watersheds in which we make our homes, knowing the waters in these regions support all of life in the area. We are grateful for this gift of life—and for the Source of All Life.—*LeAnn Blackert, Wild Church BC, BC*

SARNIA ONTARIO LAND ACKNOWLEDGMENT. *This land acknowledgment is based on one written by and with Anishinaabe elder and historian David D. Plain and shared with me to use with permission for my wild church gatherings. We created it so that it can be used in different locations.*

We acknowledge that this on which we are gathered today is part of the ancestral land of the Anishinabe. It is through their connection with the spirit of the land, water, and air that we recognize their unique cultures, traditions, and values. Together we are a treaty people; we have a shared responsibility to act with respect for the environment that sustains all life, protecting the future for those generations to come. I am an edge-walker from the Christian tradition. We come from many traditions; together, we sit in the wild church, and together, we will experience Mystery. — *Mary Abma, Wild-Edge Offerings, Sarnia, ON*

CALL TO WORSHIP AND HEALING. *This land acknowledgment was created in collaboration with local Indigenous people I know. I usually follow the acknowledgment with a call to donate funds to the Confederated Tribes of Warm Springs, a local Native group, for water and infrastructure development.*

Welcome to this place. We gather together on land of the Dog River Wasco.

Let us hear and heed the voices of all Indigenous ancestors, who have much to teach us.

Come, set aside your busyness and cares. Plant your feet firmly on this Earth and breathe deeply.

Just as in ancient times, God's Spirit is here, filling our lungs with life.

We gather along the in-chee-wanna, the Great River, and remember the deep history of those forced from these lands by treaties designed for our benefit.

We remember the Wasco, the Yakama, the Nimiipuu of the Nez Perz Nation, and the Paiute.

We remember the Cayuse, Walla Walla, and Umatilla peoples. We also remember the Ceilio Wyam and all the tribal people who still live along the in-chee-wanna, but our US government refuses to recognize them. This is a beautiful place filled with rich history and deep pain.

We come here today to worship the Creator, but our worship includes lament.

We gather today to worship and celebrate the Creator of all people, all things, and whose desire is to bring harmony, healing, and peace to our troubled histories.

We gather today to embrace all people, knowing that we are one in the heart of the One who gives life to all things.

Together, we are a living history in need of shalom. We recognize this history includes the ancients of this land who were dispossessed of their sacred places as well as their descendants who still live among us. People who have much to teach us about our Creator who dwells close to the Earth, nurturing life for all.

> *Open our ears to hear you speak.*
> *Open our eyes to see others' stories.*
> *Open our hearts to love your whole creation.*
> *Open our hands to work together for a better future for all.*
>
> —*Andy Wade, Bethel White Salmon Church,*
> *White Salmon, WA*

RELATING WITH MY OWN EARTH-HONORING ANCESTORS. When I knew I was being led to start a wild church and to practice an Earth-based spirituality, I was drawn to explore my own bloodlines and spiritual lineages. At around the same time, I had embodied and spiritual experiences of my ancestors speaking to me, welcoming me into relationship. My genealogy revealed that my lineages originate in northwest Europe and the British Isles. I knew that their ancient Earth-honoring Celtic tradition lives within me.

I immersed myself in learning as much as I could about Celtic spirituality, the history of people indigenous to those lands and how they were colonized and oppressed, and their practices, folklore, myths, and cosmologies. I name this lineage as my lens for wild church gatherings, that I walk the edges of both the Christian and pagan traditions from a Celtic worldview.

I continue to also name and grapple with my ancestors' complicity in colonization and removal of peoples indigenous to the land where I live and participation in the evils of slaveholding by some of them. I hold this tension between honoring and loving my ancestors who experienced their own dislocation and violence by European powers and also lamenting and acknowledging the harm some of them did. Through all of this, I reconnect with my most ancient ancestors, who deeply loved the particular part of the Earth where they lived; who engaged with the water, plants, and creatures as part of the divine order; and who passed this love along to me.—*Valerie Luna Serrels*

INITIATING RELATIONSHIP WITH LOCAL NATIVE PEOPLES. We were blessed at one gathering to have a couple from the Lenape Nation, whose ancestors lived on the unceded grounds where we gather. She sang a song of welcoming the spirits of her ancestors to this place as we all sat, listening in awe. We still feel their presence with us all the time.—*Sandy and John Drescher-Lehman, Fernrock Retreat Wild Church, Green Lane, PA*

EXPANDING OUR RELATIONS. We decided to start directing some of our donations to two local Indigenous groups doing land-based healing work. One of those groups has been working with our city on a project called Expanding Our Relations. It's a project to bring together people from the neighborhood around the park and Indigenous people in getting to know each other and the flora and fauna of the park. We have done some invasive plant removal and helped them with planting native medicinal plants and trees.—*Wendy Janzen, Burning Bush Forest Church, Kitchener-Waterloo, ON*

BUILDING RELATIONSHIPS. As you enter our wild church gathering space, there is a peace pole planted in a meditative rock garden. We worked with our Indigenous neighbors to honor them and include native language. Collaborating on this project helped us form personal relationships. Through these connections, we commissioned a basket from a local Indigenous basket weaver made of native ash that gets used at every wild church gathering. This year we sourced corn from the Abenaki people, who have stewarded this land for twelve thousand years. Making these personal connections has brought greater meaning to the land acknowledgments offered.—*Heather Wolfe, Wild Church, Taftsville, VT*

FOLLOWING INDIGENOUS LEADERSHIP. Our support for Indigenous autonomy on the territory where we reside has mostly involved following the leadership of Tsleil Waututh and other First Nations in direct action, ceremony, public demonstrations, letter writing, and court support in resisting the Trans-Mountain Pipeline expansion project on Burnaby Mountain and farther east.

These kinds of engagement grow our community and deepen individual and collective connection and relationship to place and to the particular plants, animals, land forms, and waterways.—*Laurel Dykstra, Salal + Cedar, Vancouver, BC*

THIN SPACE. Our wild church gathers in one of the biggest forest areas in Europe. When we started looking for "our" place, we were very well aware of the Celtic concept of a thin place. That was exactly what we looked for: a thin place in our region.

One Sunday morning, we followed a hint from a friend of ours to a hill with a small footpath through a wild forest of lime beech trees. At the top of the hill, there is a platform where birches are planted in circles. We had no idea who planted these trees in this way or why, but we immediately felt that this place has something very special for us. We learned that this hill has some caves in it where scientists found remains of humans which are more than twelve thousand years old.

So our imaginations went wild. Who might these people have been? When closing our eyes and listening into the wild, we sometimes hear in our minds voices of happy families, gathering and playing in this birch grove many thousands of years ago. Wasn't there a group over there, training younglings with slingshots for hunting? Which feasts might have happened here—celebrations of life circles like the Celtic one we as a wild church refer to? And so we connect to hills and mountains, to the wilderness, to the many cultures this place has seen, to deer and people like us who had their joyful moments, as well as tragic ones. And in our celebrations, our wanderings, our songs and poems, we realize the richness of the moment which is only a blink of an eye in the long history of this, our thin place.—*Arnd Corts, Wild Church Sauerland, Germany*

5

WILD RITUALS
Re-Placing Liturgy, Stories, and Prayers

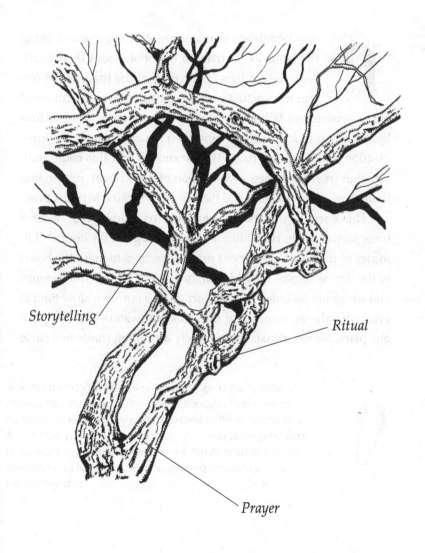

Storytelling

Ritual

Prayer

"Through practices that reacquaint people with their ecological grounding, wild church invites people into direct and interconnected relationship with the waters, trees, wildlife, hills of their own homes. They are oriented to a spirituality of place, where the natural world invites us into intimacy with the sacred. And the sacred invites us more deeply into relationship with the wild."

—*Church of the Wild*

eter Wohlleben shares some startling research about the behavior of trees in his book about their heartbeat. Researchers observed that the branches of certain trees actually change position over the course of a day—rising and falling in a regular pattern every three to four hours, by up to four inches!—and then returning to their normal position when the sun rises. They surmised that this could indicate that trees have their own version of a heartbeat, responding to the Earth's frequencies and their needs in their own slow time.

This curious, unexpected news got us wondering, "what if trees participate in ritual, like a natural liturgy of the hours?" Liturgies of the hours are ancient prayer practices to mark the hours of the day as sacred. In wild church, prayers, rituals, movements, and songs are included to transport us into our own slow time in sync with the movements of the trees and waters and beings of our place. Simple rituals like carefully arranging chairs in a circle

Most places might have all you need to create an altar. A fallen branch, sticks, a flower with broken stem, pinecones, and whatever other treasures show up. Use your imagination and bring what you have from home too—pottery, a candle (if you're able and it's not fire season) or flameless candle, cloth with a seasonal pattern, artwork, art supplies: let yourself play with ideas!

rather than in rows not only encourage conversation and decenter the leader as authority but reflect circular patterns of interconnection mirroring cycles of the seasons or orbits of the Earth and moon in relationship with each other.

RE-STORYING NEW MEANING

Earth has her own rituals, expressed in stories of glaciers, seasons, spring blossoms, anthills, wildfires, and birdsongs. As we listen with affection to the stories the land tells, we are compelled to integrate their stories into *our* stories. To remain alive, our old narratives need to be connected with new meaning particular to our geographies and context. A beloved myth or story from a sacred text or scripture carries deep wisdom that comes alive when it is reoriented to our own time and place. What was meaningful two centuries or two days ago can mean something very different in *this* moment and *this* place.

Sacred texts retold with an eco-spiritual perspective shift attention to background characters such as mountains, sea, mustard seeds, gardens, and olive branches. What roles do they play in the narrative? How can the story come alive when these so-called environmental details become central to the story rather than background? What happens when the stories are adapted to include the elements and beings alive in your ecosystem?

RITUAL IN WILD CHURCH

Many of us are accustomed to rituals being done *for* us, on our behalf, by a priest, pastor, rabbi, imam, or other holy professional. These leaders hold specific and important roles in society, but rewilding invites us to consider how we can trust our own capacity to create new rituals and adapt beloved old ones. Rewilding ancient stories so they are relevant to our own place and community requires trusting our inner authority and reclaiming our spiritual sovereignty. It is an act of resistance and healing after centuries of authoritarian religiosity.

Even though I (Valerie) have always created rituals for my kids to honor significant events, I'm not ordained, nor have I been in leadership in a church. I felt intimidated when I first considered creating rituals for our wild church gatherings. It wasn't until I stepped into that calling fully, with a strong sense of the Divine within, that I began to trust my ability to hold sacred space and ceremony with others. In my wild church, I draw from my Scots-Irish heritage to offer adaptations of ancient rituals that follow the four cross-quarter days of the seasonal Celtic festivals, plus equinox and solstice.

If the place where you meet allows fires, this can be the most direct way into ritual. Fire is itself a ritual. Humans sitting around a fire telling stories is a ritual that goes back to the beginning of our species. Sitting in silence, listening to the crackle, watching the flickering can bring one into a highly receptive state for ritual. Telling stories, playing music, drumming, singing, and fire just go together.

Creating and entering ritual space is rooted in the body and in the body of the Earth. It's rooted in rhythm and breath and presence. Whatever helps you to inhabit yourself fully, connected with the ritual movements of your place, listen to that. Listen to how the Sacred others, who have been activators of ritual for centuries, can co-create rituals with you—ancestors, fire, water, stone. Listen to your imagination, intuition, and your own practices. Below are some ways that other wild church leaders have listened, rewilded, woven, and co-created rituals for their gatherings.

A WILD INVOCATION. *This poem can serve to open a wild gathering.*

> *We gather together in this wild cathedral*
> *where there are no walls or windows*
> *to separate us*
> *from the land on which*
> *trees breathe and plants transform*
> *the sunlight*
> *where the spirited elements dance and desire,*
> *tousle our hair*
> *and play on our skin,*
> *where everlasting cycles of birth and death,*
> *and birth again,*
> *are engraved in the seasons'*
> *turnings.*
> *With abundant gratitude and openness,*
> *quieted hearts and wandering souls,*
> *we pay attention*
> *as our senses reveal their ancient knowing,*
> *and call this*
> *sacred.*

> —*Mary Abma, Wild-Edge Offerings, Bright's Grove, ON*

OPENING PRAYER. *A prayer to open a service.*

Let us turn our hearts toward this world with love. Allow our hearts to break with the pain of the world. Fill our hearts with the light of love and beauty. We pray for the fierce commitment to hold the grief in one hand and the joy in the other. We pray for the tender compassion to listen to the voices of those who are suffering. We center the light of our hearts on those who have overlooked and forgotten, those in our human community and our more-than-human kin who are filled with fear and regret and despair, as well as those voices within ourselves that are overlooked and hiding in shadow. We pray that the love of God, the presence of angels and beings of light, and love be present here with us. We declare that this is sacred space. Father, Mother, Sister, Brother. Kin. Amen.—*Victoria Loorz*

INVOCATION OF THE WATERSHED. *This invocation was created for my own ecosystem. Research the creatures, land forms, and waters in your ecosystem. One person reads the regular type; all read the bolded type.*

We open to sacred relationship with the beings in the ecosystem that is unique to [*name the place*], acknowledging the divine mystery alive in all beings.

To the soil, small pebbles, and multishaped stones who make up the ground we stand on and the giant slabs of rock that create these ancient mountains: *thank you for reminding us of the importance of grounding ourselves.*

To the fast-flowing creeks and slow-moving rivers that flow through the canyons and floors of this mountain range: *thank you for reminding us of the flow that is life.*

To the many species of pine and hardwood trees, shrubs, flowering plants, and mycelium rooted and growing in this forest: *thank you for reminding us of our own rootedness and growth.*

To the rabbits, raccoons, foxes, and bears and to all species of mammals who build homes and roam through this forest: *thank you for reminding us we, too, are animal.*

To the blue jays, finches, crows, and to all flying species who nest and migrate through this forest: *thank you for reminding us of our limitless nature.*

To the brook trout, bass, and sunfish who spawn in and navigate the creeks and rivers that run through these canyons and the forest floor: *thank you for reminding us there is life beneath the surface.*

To the frogs and salamanders and all species of amphibian and reptile who hop, walk, and slither through this forest: *thank you for reminding us of the value of diversity.*

To the butterflies, beetles, spiders, and all species of insect who crawl, bury, and weave through this forest home: *thank you for reminding us that small things create worlds.*

From the smallest plant fiber to the largest outcropping of mountain, we honor you. —*Valerie Luna Serrels*

EARTH EUCHARIST. *This Eucharist is adapted from Episcopal priest Stephen Blackmer, a wild church leader in New Hampshire. It is approached from the perspective that we are part of a communion of creation. God created us to be in an interconnected relationship with all life. At Burning Bush Forest Church, when we celebrate communion together, we offer the first piece of bread back to the earth and the last drops of wine or juice back to the earth.*

[*Place bread and wine on your altar, which could be the earth, a stump, or a rock.*]

From before time, God made ready the creation. The Divine Spirit moved over the deep and brought all things into being: sun, moon, and stars; earth, winds, and waters; rock, fire, and every living thing. Today we join with all the Earth and heavens in a chorus of praise that rings through eternity. We remember our oneness with all that exists and all that has life and that it is a joyful thing to be in God's presence with each other, with this land, and with all creation.

This meal we are about to share is a miracle and a mystery—a gift of earth, water, wind, and fire and of seeds buried in the earth and cracked open. This bread and this juice, with their many meanings, are gifts of life to the living. For followers of Jesus, these gifts assume particular meaning. Jesus broke bread with those who were outcast, healed those who were sick, and proclaimed good news to those who were poor. He yearned to draw all of the world into the heart of God. When Jesus's life was nearing its end, Jesus was eating supper with his friends. He took bread, gave thanks, broke it, and shared it, saying, "Take, eat: This is my body, offered to heal the whole world. Whenever you eat it, remember me." [Break bread.]

And as supper was ending, Jesus took a cup of wine. Again he gave thanks and offered it to his friends, saying, "Drink this, all of you: This is the cup of the new covenant—a promise of eternal love poured out for you and for all beings. Whenever you drink it, remember this." [Pour cup.]

Here, with the Earth as our altar, we savor God with all of our senses. As we eat and drink together, we get to taste, smell, and touch the Sacred. We are reminded that we are one with God, with each other, and with all creation. Before we eat and drink, let's pray: Divine Love, pour out your Spirit upon these gifts. Fill us with your breath, O God, opening our eyes and renewing us in your love. Send your Spirit over this land and over the whole Earth, making everything a new creation. Amen.

[Hold a piece of bread and the cup.]

These are the gifts of God for all the creatures of God.

Remembering that Jesus came to renew us and the whole world, we will offer the first piece of bread and the last drops of juice to the earth. [*Place the piece of bread on the earth.*]

Come, eat and drink, one and all, whoever hungers and thirsts for renewal. All are welcome.

[*Invite people forward to receive a piece of bread and a cup of juice. Ask someone to help with serving the bread and/or cup. After all have been served, pour some of the wine or juice onto the earth.*]

Our God of abundance has fed us with the bread of life and the cup of love. With deep appreciation and thanks for the communion we share with each other and with the Earth, we pray: Eternal Spirit, Earth-maker, Life-giver, Pain-bearer, source of all that is and ever shall be, you have showered us with abundance. With the food we need for today, feed us. For the hurt we cause, forgive us. As we lose our way, restore us. Enlarge within us the sense of fellowship with all living creatures, all part of the family of God. Tune our hearts to live in harmony with Christ, with the Earth, with all creatures, and with our human neighbors too. Now and forever. Amen.—*Wendy Janzen, Burning Bush Forest Church, Kitchener-Waterloo, ON*

AN ECOLOGICAL STATIONS OF THE CROSS. Since 2016, Salal + Cedar has hosted an Ecological Stations of the Cross during Holy Week: an annual connection of the Christian faith story, specifically the crucifixion, with the suffering of creation. We meet outdoors, usually in a location that is troubled by environmental harms. Different individuals and communities prepare and host stations of five to ten minutes each—stations that draw parallels between the last days and hours before Easter and elements in our climate and extinction crises. Offerings have included litanies, songs, body prayers, physical/sacramental acts, and direct action and often have a liturgical element of call and response.

LITURGICAL BACKGROUND. Stations of the Cross are a Good Friday tradition of prayer and contemplation on a series of images depicting the events from the time that Jesus is arrested to his burial. We hope to keep this contemplative tone.

ECOLOGICAL BACKGROUND. We ask folks preparing stations to consider local concerns (such as pipelines, loss of particular local species, local and global connections, climate change, displacement of Indigenous people). Themes include repentance, culpability, betrayal, complicity, empire, suffering, compassion, power/powerlessness, death, lament, longing, despair, outrage, hope, and hopelessness. Stations can include silence, poetry, movement, song, action, scripture (from the passion narratives or elsewhere). They could be shaped around a concrete event like arrest, trial, death, or burial, but they don't have to be. We begin with a territorial acknowledgment and round of introductions (names, pronouns, access needs) and follow a roughly chronological order from courts to tomb, but each year has different offerings. A typical service has five to eight stations and ends with a fairly solemn and silent dispersal.

EXAMPLE FROM ONE OF THE STATIONS: JESUS CARRIES THE CROSS. Several of us led a group of about thirty down the trail to the first station to a gentle drumbeat, reminding us of the living heartbeat of Mother Earth. There we gathered near a salmon creek by a small wooden footbridge. Land acknowledgments and a short prayer were offered. I suggested a parallel among Jesus's struggle on his journey to the crucifixion, our struggle for ecological and social justice, and the salmon's struggle upstream to death and new birth. After a moment of quiet reflection, we led people in the song "We Stand on Guard for Thee" and then offered these reflections for our first station:

We stand for the salmon, we stand for the eagle,
We stand for the cedar, we stand for the people,
Salmon, eagle, cedar, people, we stand on guard for thee.
We stand for the children, we stand for the elders,
We stand for creation, we stand for each nation,
Children, elders, creation, each nation, we stand on guard for thee.
We stand with our sisters, we stand with our brothers,
We stand for our families, we stand for each other,
Sisters, brothers, families, each other, we stand on guard
for thee.
We stand for the salmon, we stand for the eagle,
We stand for the cedar, we stand for the people,
Salmon, eagle, all our relations, we stand on guard for thee.
We praise you, Creator, for these! We praise you, Creator,
for these!

We then gave each person a small piece of copper wire that they could use to shape into a fish or other symbol of their choice. People could keep them or share them or leave them along the way in a special place or whatever they chose. The service then includes a time for ecological reflection, lament, and an embodied reflection. The next entry contains a sample of a lament prayer used in one of these events. —*Laurel Dykstra, Salal + Cedar, Vancouver, BC*

PRAYER OF LAMENT IN SEVEN VOICES. *The following text can be written on four-by-six cards and read by seven voices in the circle.*

We are without words to express this profound loss for Musqueam (xʷməθkʷiỷəm), stewards of this land from time immemorial. As settlers, we accept responsibility for this wrongdoing.

Voice 1: Some say the Earth is the Lord's, but it is destined to become private property.

Voice 2: Some say the Earth is "our mother," and yet we take from the Earth without offering thanksgiving.

Voice 3: The Earth is sacred, and the land is our life, but we continue to exploit and destroy.

Voice 4: Can we maintain covenant treaty relationships for "as long as the sun shines, the grass grows, and the rivers flow"?

Voice 5: Create in me a clean heart, O God. Unsettle my soul and renew a right spirit within me.

Voice 6: Unquiet me to shout this story's whispers.

Voice 7: So that I won't settle for less than your kingdom come on Earth as it is in heaven. —*Laurel Dykstra, Salal + Cedar, Vancouver, BC*

A CEREMONY FOR TREES BEING REMOVED. I was asked to lead a ceremony to honor the lives of two trees that needed to be cut down. We gathered in a circle before the trees, and I led those who were gathered to begin by noticing our breath, acknowledging the gift of oxygen provided by the trees and our gift to them of carbon dioxide. We shared stories about these trees, welcoming all emotions. I invited the group to speak their gratitude to the trees who were being cut down. Then I read a poem, "When I Am Among Trees," by Mary Oliver, and poured water at the base of the tree as an offering of gratitude. We walked back to the third tree on the lot, which will remain. There we sat in a circle once again and ended with a song of blessing.—*Mindy Braun, Wild Journey, Santa Rosa, CA*

A GRIEF LITURGY. *I wrote this liturgy for an Ash Wednesday in the Ashes ceremony after the Thomas Fire in Ojai, California, that burned 300,000 acres. Billions of creatures lost their lives in terror. Nobody had been talking about the impact on the other-than-humans. So we created a list of local people groups, creatures, geographies, and climates that have been devastated by changing weather patterns or destruction. A version of this ritual could be used on Ash Wednesday, Earth Day, or any time you choose to honor the layers of loss we are facing. Creating group rituals to name and process grief is an important part of this time of extinctions, environmental destruction, and climate disruption. It's important to list as many local creatures in your context as possible: to honor them, and to see and hear the long list of those who have died. Listing every creature who is endangered or has gone extinct is an important and powerful ritual for any grief gathering, evoking our emotional connection with them. One person reads the regular type; the group reads the words in bold.*

In the cry of the prophet Joel . . . in the wake of climate disaster, the land is devastated . . . *We have no words.*

When desert wind displaces fog, when embers fall instead of rain, the land is devastated . . . *We have no words.*

When flames devour canyons and meadows, riverbeds and mountains, leaping past firefighters, faster than animals can run or fly, the land is devastated . . . *We have no words.*

When the night flares orange, and terror strikes mule deer, black bear, quail, and skunk; mountain lion, jackrabbit, tree frogs, and goldfinch; garter snakes, fence lizards, tiger salamanders, arroyo toads; slider turtles, roadrunners, kestrels and kingbirds; lark sparrows, woodpeckers, flycatchers, bluebirds, egrets, herons, towhees, scrub jays, mallards, hawks, eagles, ticks, and gnats; condors, monarchs, coots, and hummingbirds; mergansers, orioles, meadowlarks, and wrens; robins, thrushes, phoebes, and swallows; buntings, grosbeaks, warblers, and pond turtles; martins, blackbirds, mourning doves, and owls; ravens, wild boar, crows, and weasels; coyote, king snakes, chipmunks, and raccoons; rainbow trout, millipedes, black widows, and scorpions; skippers, silk moths, hedgehogs, and blues; checkerspots, swallowtails, beetles, and possum; red fox, bluegill, dragonflies, and bumblebees; grasshoppers, cabbage moths, brown bats, and gophers; bobcats, cottontails, ground squirrels, and wasps; ladybugs, crickets, water striders, and crayfish; western toad, red-legged frog, CA newt, and rattlesnake: the land is devastated . . . *We have no words.*

When engines devour beauty, apathy eats the poor, profits drive power, and consumption explodes the wild, the land is devastated . . . *We have no words.*

When what we love is ashes, the winds bring little rain, our taxes fuel insanity, the land and our hearts are devastated . . . *We have no words.*

[*Pause for a long silence.*]

And into this no-words, we listen. — *Lisa Dahill, written for Ojai Church of the Wild, Ojai, CA*

INVOCATION OF GRIEF. *This invocation invites us to approach the devastating personal, ecological, and collective grief within and around us as an act of reverence and interconnection. We do not enter alone. We enter through these gates of grief as a community into a wider field of belonging.*

We invoke our ancestors with whom we are interconnected to help hold and release our grief. May we know and experience their closeness. *For the veil is thin.*

We invoke a thinning of the spaces between us and the rest of the alive world, both visible and invisible. Our kindred allies— the animals, trees and water worlds, the plant and stone kin, the elementals, the planetary and cosmic guardians, and the allies and guardians of the invisible realms—to help hold and release our grief. May we know and experience their closeness. *For the veil is thin.*

We invoke a thinning of the places within us where there are inner blockages, traumas, densities of energy, and thick boundaries of protection and offer our gratitude for the wisdom of our bodies to protect us. We place our trust in the Source of all of life that lives within us, too, to allow the thick boundaries around our hearts to soften. *For the veil is thin.*

When we open to grief, the neurochemicals in our brain dance in a new pattern that slows down some functionality. So we invoke the intelligence of our bodies and the Source of all intelligence to re-pattern our neurology in our grieving. *For the veil is thin.*

May we walk into the sacred thin spaces of grief accompanied by our own wisdom and a whole ecosystem of wisdom, through the land beneath our feet, our intuitive awareness, and the presence of the Infinite. *For the veil is thin.* —*Valerie Luna Serrels*

A PRAYER OF HONOR. Under the shade of a giant live oak tree, we complete a circle and build a little altar with a cloth I made, along with leaves, stones, and sticks we collect nearby. I set out a glass jar of communion juice made from the wild blackberries and apples someone brought from their backyard tree. The children and teens scramble into the arms of the ancient tree through her ladder of branches. They listen with intermittent giggles from above as we begin the service with silence, listening to the beings who worship daily in this place, and simple invocation that acknowledges with gratitude the Native peoples who have tended this land for generations, the sacred presence of the trees and the creatures who invite us into worship with them. We end the prayer: "In learning to honor the holiness in the others who are not human, may we learn to honor the sacred within ourselves and in all peoples. May we honor one another and honor life itself and sacred Mystery, Christ within all things, holding us all together, amen."—*Victoria Loorz*

EMBODIED MUSIC-MAKING WITH NATURE. Making music is a fundamental part of our wild church gathering. It is an embodied act. Our hands clap, our vocal cords vibrate, we sway from our torsos and tap our feet. Live music pulls us out of our mental states and puts us back into our bodies, where we have a better chance of reconnecting with the natural world. For many of us, the word *music* is closely associated with ideas of talent and skill: qualitative ideas of good and bad. But every human alive has a heartbeat and therefore lives with rhythm, the foundation of most musical ideas. Nature, too, has music: the runs and trills of birdsong, the crystalline melodies of water in streams, the deep bass notes of trees moving against each other in the wind.

As musicians in wild church gatherings, our task is to facilitate a connection between human participants and the embodied music that is their birthright. We start gatherings with the drums, a connection to our heartbeat and the heartbeat of many creatures rustling through the forest around us. Human participants are gently encouraged to pick up a percussion instrument and join the drumming, and inevitably we end up in a common rhythm, moving and creating sound as one.

Music works best when it adapts to its environment. We choose songs that are simple, with lyrics that suit the gathering, our forest hosts, and often the theme. The container of the gathering is a communal and changing entity, so if the flow of the gathering is leading us in a direction where a song doesn't make sense, we don't use it. We close most gatherings with everyone singing a simple and familiar song or chant, our bodies creating a sound together that reminds us of our unity and creatureliness as we head back into the world. And sometimes, when we're very lucky, a deer will come toward our gathering, seemingly drawn by our song. —*Amy Moffitt, Wild Earth Spiritual Community, Washington, DC*

STONE STORIES. *I asked the participants to find or bring a stone and then shared the following:*

If you brought a stone with you, take it out and hold it. Feel its heft, its shape, its texture. Think of where it came from, where you picked it up. Was it a beach, a creek, a construction site, a backyard, a quarry, a roadside? A healthy place, a threatened place, a degraded place? Think of your stone's long story, its endurance. And think about how it may speak to you of endurance for yourself and for the community of environmental care we are part of, locally and globally. When we return, we'll place our stones together to make a cairn. In placing our stones, we recognize that we stand in a long tradition of care for the Earth that spans all ages, all cultures, all faiths; we acknowledge all who have gone before us. And we commit an act of hope—I would say, an act of radical hope: that we will not be the last to walk this way, that there will be future generations who will follow in our steps.—*Laurel Dykstra, Salal + Cedar, Vancouver, BC*

A GAIAN READING OF 1 CORINTHIANS 12:12–31. *A retelling of a scripture from an eco-spiritual lens.*

For in the one Spirit we were all created into one body—Jew or Gentile, all faith traditions or no faith traditions; of all genders; of all languages; of all colors—Black, brown, white skin, green and multicolored scaly skin, fur, feathers, stems, flowers, and roots; two-legged, four-legged, multilegged, legless, winged, finned, and rooted; all creatures, minerals, and elements of land, sea, and sky.

Indeed, the body does not consist of one member but of many diverse members! If the tree would say, "Because I am not a human, I do not belong to the body," that would not make it any less a part of the body. And if the river would say, "Because I am not an eagle, I do not belong to the body," that would not make it any less a part of the body. If the whole body were a tree, where would the sense of ambulation be? If the whole body were a human, where would the sense of roots moving through the earth be?

But as it is, the Source-of-All-That-Is arranged the members in the body, each one of them, as they chose. The head cannot say to the mountaintop, "I have no need of you," nor again the heart to the butterfly, "I have no need of you." But the Mystery of Life has so arranged the body, giving great honor to those deemed inferior, that there may be no dissension within the body, but all members may have equal care for one another.

If one member suffers, all suffer together with it; if one member is honored, all rejoice together with it.—*Valerie Luna Serrels*

MAKING A BEAUTY OFFERING. My wild church has been informed by both my training as a pastor of United Church of Christ churches for fifteen years and my training over the past three years by South American shamanism. I adapted this offering from my mentors in Peru.

To make a beauty offering, spend some time before your gathering finding a beautiful gift from the natural world. In the Andes, this most basic, regularly made offering is called 'K'intu and is made with three coca leaves, a sacred plant. We've used flowers and native plant seeds. The intentional seeking of the gift is a ritual in itself. Take the time to contemplatively focus on your beloved (the place where you'll gather) and ask what might please them. Consider the difference: between searching for a gift for someone you love that they would really enjoy and stopping at the gas station on the way to a birthday party to pick up a last-minute gift.

When making the offering, present it with words or even song, with intentionality and explicit gratitude. Speaking the words, however softly, is an important part of the conversation, as are gestures like holding the offering elements up and even waving them with small hand movements. Here's something I've said before: "Come, come, Spirit, as you soak this place with your presence. This is for you and all present in this forest. Thank you for your life and embracing me in this place. With gratitude and love, I bring you this gift. In response to your love and embrace, I bring you this gift. I am in need of peace and clarity about my next step on my journey. Please come and help me."

Finally, surrender the offering to the land: bury the gift, scatter the ashes to the wind, pour the water, place it on your tree stump altar, or simply place it in a place where it won't be disturbed, like between rocks. I say something simple like "Thank you. This is for you."—*Greg Turk, Wild Sacred, Seattle, WA*

ELEMENTAL PRAYER. *This prayer of gratitude draws our awareness to the four elements of matter.*

We give thanks this day
for the sun, moon, and stars lighting our way,
illuminating beauty, energizing all life.
We give thanks this day for the ground beneath us,
solid rock and living soil,
foundation and fertility,
supporting and sustaining.
We give thanks this day for the water of life,
rain and rivers,
oceans and glaciers,
flowing and hydrating.
We give thanks this day for sky,
air, and wind, animating breath,
sacred interchange, inspiring and connecting.
For all four elements and the ways they work together,
for all creatures,
for all places,
for life and death,
we offer our deepest gratitude
to Creator of all.

—Wendy Janzen, Burning Bush Forest Church,
Kitchener-Waterloo, ON

INVITING OUR INNER SILENCE. *A prayer like this can draw on the specifics of your place. What does your group hear when you are outside and silent?*

> As we settle into stillness, our senses heighten, and slowly we
> begin to perceive

*the thrum of bumblebee vibrations, droning in the
autumn chill,*
> *the rustle of sparrows in the dry, crackling undergrowth*
> *the swish of tall prairie grasses as they bend under the brisk,*
north wind
> *the vibration of the wild goose's wings as they lift the lithe*
birds into airstreams
> *the needlepoint of a mosquito's insistence*
> *the scent of fresh earth, humus, and decay*
> *the fresh taste of crisp, October air and its promise of apples,*
> *the greys, blues, and greens of the lake,*
> *stirred by crashing whitecaps and bathed in swirling sand,*
> *the scolding of the squirrel preparing for winter, and*
> *the dazzle of sunshine through raindrops that linger on*
the leaves.

> *And beyond the five senses that we take for granted,*
> *we feel the "more" that we cannot name*
> *where the limits of our language leave us mute*
> *and we sense with our whole being*
> *and enter into the mystery.*
> > > —*Mary Abma, Wild-Edge Offerings,*
> > > *Bright's Grove, ON*

A GRACE PRAYER. *A prayer for grace that can be prayed at any point in a wild church gathering.*

> *May the grace of the trees with their green leaves and deep
> roots be with you,*

May the grace of the elements (fire, water, earth, and air) be with you,
    May the grace of the unseen world be with you,
    May the love of wild places remain in your heart.

—*Dana Jefferson, Allegheny Cathedral of the Wild, Huntingdon, PA*

6

EARTH CYCLES
Reorienting to the Rhythm of the Wild

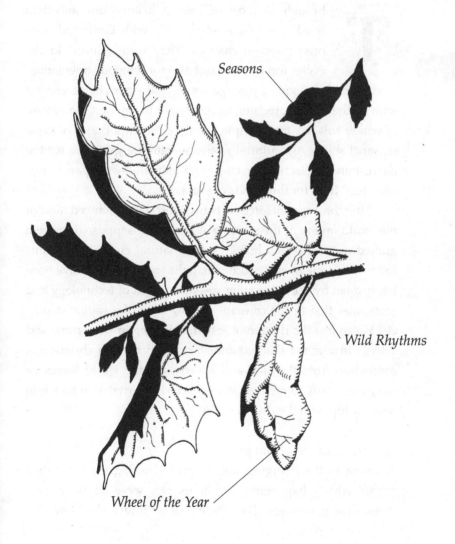

Seasons

Wild Rhythms

Wheel of the Year

"Even a simple gaze at a full moon can be a spiritual experience if you are mindful enough. And a glorious sunset can summon hallelujahs from deep in your soul. Humans are made to engage in life-affirming conversation with the whole, holy web of life."

—*Church of the Wild*

 hroughout most of human history, our ancestors lived in intimate relationship with Earth and honored seasonal changes. They were attuned to the cycles for survival and also for religious orientation. Ancient burial mounds, passage tombs, and stone circles, erected with mathematical precision to allow light to enter on the sunrise of winter solstice, for example, speak of the importance of these seasonal shifts. Agricultural festivals—offering gratitude for the harvest and protection for crops and animals—were part of our ancestors' lives for thousands of years.

After the imperial forces of church and state colonized most of the world, many of these seasonal festivals disappeared or were grafted onto Christian holidays. Our natural circadian rhythms follow the cycle of sun and moon, light and dark, but have been interrupted by the exhausting speed and light of technology and economies tied to the constant surging flow of a capitalist society. We've lost the rhythm of rest and slowing in wintertime and activity in summer that our ancestors practiced. Our chronic disconnection from the land and aliveness of the world leaves us dangling, adrift, unmoored. Wild church is an invitation back into relationship with the rhythms of life.

SEASONS MIRROR WITHIN US

Attuning to the changing seasons and honoring the ways they mirror what's happening within us can serve as organizing themes for gatherings. The wisdom of autumn's shedding and winter's dormancy invites us to remember that our body needs seasons for rest and solitude. Enthusiastically greeting the spring flowers as they appear attunes us to the new growth within that is longing for expression. Meeting outside throughout the year—in heat and mud, snow and rain—reconnects us with the rhythms of Earth. Through a wild church, we become more regulated with the rhythms of the changing seasons, with all kinds of weather, and with the erratic and changing climate.

Weather patterns are seasonal rituals spoken by Earth and her relationship with sky, atmosphere, and human activity. Careful attention to weather informs not simply the logistics or decisions around canceling a gathering. Each weather pattern has its own wisdom to share if we are listening. Attuning ourselves to the elements of weather, we listen for the wisdom each rainfall and gentle breeze holds, what warnings come in the voices of hurricanes or flooding.

As the Earth's rhythms become more unbalanced and dysregulated, we notice an echo within ourselves. How do the more extreme and erratic weather systems impact our moods, emotions, and energy levels? Are we picking up on not only our own groanings but those of the Earth? Naming this interconnection opens space for conversation around our responses to the radical changes in the climate.

The cycles of seasons are mirrored in the recurring theme of exile and return found throughout many sacred stories. The pattern of life, death, and resurrection is more than a religious concept. It is embedded in all aspects of life: cycles of summer into autumn into winter into spring, daylight into night and back again, love lost and grieved and cracking open to love again. The patterns of our personal lives are not independent from the cycles of all of life.

Equinox and solstice aren't just positional changes of the Earth outside of us. They hold tremendous cyclical energies that

Honor your safety and the safety of others—not your need for comfort. If it's unsafe to drive, cancel or postpone. If it's just rainy, cold, or hot, gather anyway, even if it's for a shorter time than your regular gatherings. Our cultural addiction to comfort disconnects us from the rhythms of weather.

correspond with our human experience. Earth's rebalance of light and dark at the equinoxes invites us to tune in to what needs rebalancing within us. Remembering that we are connected with the turning of the seasons and cyclical shifts invites us to rejoin a sacred rhythm we share with all life.

STORIES & PRACTICES

IDEAS FOR HOLY DAYS. To celebrate Earth Day, participants gathered fallen items from the ground during their wandering and brought them back to our circle, where we created a nature mandala (inspired by a practice in the book *Morning Altars*). Earth altars are a beautiful way of honoring many occasions. On Mother's Day, we acknowledged the many different ways of mothering without giving birth (mothering our inner child, siblings, parents, our ecosystem, the children of others, animals, and those who are sick, elderly, or vulnerable). For Valentine's Day, I made raw chocolate with rose petals and rose flower essence to share. On Imbolc, we celebrated seeds and the seeding of intentions. Around Thanksgiving, I like to share the Haudenosaunee Thanksgiving Address, and to honor All Saints' Day, we bring photos or objects significant to a deceased loved one to our altar.—*Tamara Grenier, Lowcountry Wild Church, Charleston / Johns Island, SC*

WILD CHURCH IN A RAINSTORM. We gathered in an invigorating storm in March. Our watershed was experiencing much rain and some flooding. We gathered with umbrellas in our usual circle. It was windy and cold too. Our gathering was a bit shorter than usual, yet people didn't want to cut it too short. We still gathered in the circle for some readings and reflections, wandered for about twenty minutes, and then returned to the circle to share our experience. Being with the storm felt invigorating and cleansing. After years of drought, there was also so much celebration with the Earth for the much-needed rain.—*Mindy Braun, Wild Journey, Santa Rosa, CA*

SUMMER SOLSTICE RITUAL. I once brought the myth of Prometheus as the centerpiece story and ritual for a summer solstice gathering, welcoming back the full force of the sun. This ancient Greek creation story tells about the Titan trickster, Prometheus, stealing the fire from the gods to bring it to humans and the suffering that went with that choice. This myth highlights our primary relationship with the sacred element of fire and sun as both the survival of our species and the symbol of the rise of human consciousness as well as the danger this represents to the powers that be.

We gathered our chairs in a circle around a ceremonially lit fire and told stories about how our earliest, deepest origin story goes back to fire and the big bang, from unity and singularity to separation and the necessary division of elements and chemicals that would become everything that is. How fire set the human species on their evolutionary trajectory and this ancient ritual of telling stories around fires is in our blood. The telling of the Prometheus myth was accompanied by drumming and rhythm instruments, which added a more experiential and embodied way of digesting the story. We opened up the space for communal drumming and then sharing around our relationship with fire and our inner sun.—*Valerie Luna Serrels*

BLESSING OF THE ANIMALS PRAYER. *We follow the Lutheran liturgical calendar for the Blessing of the Animals on the Feast of St. Francis (often the first Sunday in October). Here is a prayer we say.*

Creator God, you made all there is and gave life to all who live. Thank you for this beautiful and life-giving Earth. Thank you for all the people and all our brother and sister creatures who live on this planet with us. We stand here in your beautiful creation and are blessed by it and by all that live on this land. We in turn bless this place and all that live here: the birds, mammals, reptiles, and insects; the trees, grasses, plants, fungi, and molds. We also bless the animals that we have brought with us to worship today. Thank you for our animal companions. Help us be a blessing to them as they are to us. Amen.—*Carmen Retzlaff, founder of New Life Lutheran Church, a Wild Church*

WINTER WEATHER WANDERING. We gather in rain or snow as long as it is safe. Our first fully drenching rainstorm resulted in us canceling our gathering because even driving conditions were hazardous. For another, lighter rainfall, we brought a tarp. Typically, we must walk a little way to find our spot in the woods, but we wanted to be able to see folks as they walked toward us in case the mud caused a mishap, so we set up the tarp within view of parking. We assumed no one would show up, yet six or seven of us gathered under the noisy tarp. You really have to speak loud over a barrage of rain on plastic! We leaned in close, reflected out loud, and sat in silence.

When it came time for the wander, I thought, *No one is going to walk in this mess!* Friends, never underestimate wild ones! When the bell was rung to begin our wandering, every single person stood up and walked away from the covering. They stayed out for twenty minutes, returning thoroughly soaked. Most interesting to me is that the sharing was particularly enlivened, as though the rain had awakened our slumbering senses and brought it all into greater intensity.—*Sarah Anders, Wild Earth Spiritual Community, Washington, DC*

RAINY DAY WANDERING. At a late spring gathering, dark clouds rolled in quickly, and a heavy rainstorm developed. We ran to the picnic shelter and lit a fire to continue. During the wandering, some found a place to sit under the shelter where they could connect with a tree or plant from a short distance. Several went out into the rain. One young woman decided to run out without a raincoat, just for the experience of it. This wasn't like her. She even took off her shoes and walked in the mud near the river's edge. She said she wasn't expecting this but that it felt like a state of bliss and that she experienced the mud as sacred.—*Valerie Luna Serrels*

ADVENT SPIRAL. We meet at night during Advent and set up fire pits, Swedish torches, and ice lanterns around a spiral garden. Evergreen boughs, a symbol of the tree of life, and apples, representing the seed of new life and hidden potential, are set in the center of the spiral as an altar. Each person is invited, one at a time, to follow the lit spiral path, visiting five stations of Advent: Hope. Peace. Joy. Love. Christ.—*Heather Wolfe, Wild Church, Taftsville Chapel, VT*

THE LONGEST NIGHT BONFIRE. This has become Wild Church Cincinnati's signature service, drawing the largest number of participants every year. We hold it in a clearing behind a local

United Methodist Church, deep enough in the woods to be obscured from traffic. It always occurs on December 21 and is a time to center into the coming darkness, then rejoice that the longest night will be followed by community dinner and the breaking of bread. Homemade soups, breads, and desserts are offered at a community meal following the bonfire. At the first bonfire we held, we allowed grief at the injury of a beloved community member to be expressed, then gave color-changing fire packets to all who expressed that grief. As the flames flickered different colors, the mood lifted, and we rejoiced in one another's company and the knowledge that while there is weeping in the night, joy will surely follow in the morning.—*Janet Steele, Wild Church Cincinnati, Cincinnati, OH*

WINTER PAUSE. We take a winter pause from our monthly services due to ice and cold. This pausing and resting reflects much of the reality of the natural world during this time. We don't gather in person for the months of January, February, and March. This past winter, we decided to hold an online book group to stay connected.—*Diane Anderson, Chapel in the Pines, Wellesley, MA*

WINTER SOLSTICE. *Here is a winter solstice ritual that we have developed. You will need three candles per person.*

Winter Solstice is the longest night and the shortest day of the year for us. It is an annual cycle that our ancestors knew well. It was a time to party, pray, and reflect. They lit fires. Gathered together. Toasted life. Named the dark. Summoned the light. Human cultures all around the globe noted these shifts. Winter Solstice is a time to hibernate. To minimize effort. To grow below the surface. Thank you for joining together to do as our ancestors did: notice, name, and mark this season of the long night.

Sit in a circle with three or more candles for each person set up in the middle. Reflect on the meaning of this night: in astronomy, nature, and your life. Share around the circle what each person would like less of in the coming year. After they share, they blow out a candle. When all the candles are extinguished, I will say, "Sit. In. The. Dark. Take. It. In."

Breathe. Notice the pause between breaths. Share in quiet conversation about what happens in the dark that doesn't happen in the light.

Light one candle and begin to share around the circle again. This time, reflecting on what each would like more of in the coming year. Light a candle from the lit candle. [*Allow time for people to share.*]

Now, after everyone has shared, it's time for a party! — *Beth Amsbury, Gathering Ground, Seattle, WA*

THE WHEEL OF THE YEAR. After offering monthly Church of the Wild gatherings for a few years, I transitioned to gatherings that follow the Celtic Wheel of the Year only, which means we only gather eight times during the year. We've been meeting on the Sunday closest to the solstice, equinox, and cross-quarter festivals. For the ancient Celts, the four primary cross-quarter days were fire festivals that developed within the context of their planting, harvesting, hunting, and dormant seasons. Within a Celtic cosmology, the beginning of the year was Samhain. Here's the basic framework of the four cross-quarter festivals.

Samhain (October 31 / November 1) marks the end of summer and harvest and the descent of winter and the beginning of a new year. Connection: death, what is ready to be let go of, honoring ancestors, grief-tending. Altars usually have photos or mementos of ancestors that participants bring, along with ashes, sticks, or stones.

Imbolc / St. Brigid's Day (February 1) marks the beginning of spring and translates to "in the belly." Reaffirming the cycle of life and rebirth. Associated with the goddess Brigid and the woman St. Brigid and the divine feminine, it is now an official holiday in Ireland in honor of St. Brigid. We decorate an altar with Brigid crosses made from reeds, icons or statues of Brigid or the divine feminine, a bowl of holy water, and a candle.

Beltane (May 1) is recognized by the Celts as the beginning of summer: the light half of the year, marriage, and fertility. The word *Beltane* translates as "bright fire" and is associated with "fire of Bel," after Belenus, the Celtic god of the sun, fire, healing, and prophecy. At our wild church, we focus on fire and what is fertile and ready to be grown within us. We decorate an altar with flowers and symbols of growth or fertility.

Lúnasa (August 1)—Lughnasadh, Lughnasa, or Lúnasa—is Irish for "August" and means the "assembly of Lugh," a god of Irish mythology. It marks the beginning of the harvest. At our gatherings, we invite participants to bring some bounty from their gardens for the altar. The practices and rituals are focused on noticing what growth within is being harvested in one's life or in the world.—*Valerie Luna Serrels*

SAMHAIN GATHERING WITH SILENT SUPPER. I offer a contemplative service each year to honor the Celtic tradition of Samhain, a time when the veil between worlds is thin. We gather around a fire in our local park that has fireplaces and picnic tables under a shelter.

Invocation. We begin with contemplative songs, land acknowledgments, prayers, and the story of Samhain and call in our ancestors. In ancient times, Samhain marked the end of the year and of the harvest season. Fires would be lit on the hilltops, and the bones of livestock would be burned (hence the word *bonfire*, which means "fire of the bones.") to protect the land and crops. Ancestors were remembered, and preparations were made for the dark half of the year. The old hearth fire was blown out and a new one lit from the communal fire, marking the beginning of a new year.

Silent Supper. Candles are lit, and an ancestor altar is set up in this space. I offer a prayer something like this: "I invite all of our ancestors and lineages to be present. To be welcomed and remembered. As we eat this food, we offer gratitude for the nourishment of courage, love, resilience, and fortitude they developed to allow us to be here today. And we recognize the wounds and trauma they carried in their lifetimes that then was passed along to others. We pray for healing within ourselves for the wounds we carry, to end cycles of trauma."

Food is set out, potluck style, and we sit down to eat in silence. Music can be played. At each table, there is an empty chair where food is placed for a departed loved one. I invite people to bring forward mementos, photos, or symbols of their departed loved ones.

Fire Circle and Myth Telling. Drummers begin to drum, and we move to the fire circle. I share a story, myth, or poem about fire, ancestors, or endings.

Ritual and Wandering. As people listen to the drumming and gaze at the flames, I make pens and strips of paper available and invite people to write one thing that they mourn about a particular ancestor or their lineage and one thing they are grateful for. Or something they are feeling called to release. Allowing five to ten minutes for this, I then invite a thirty-minute silent solo wandering, imagining that one or more of your ancestors are with you.

Gathering in Council / Sharing. Each person is invited to stand and share their story, along with their photo or memento from the altar, before releasing their paper strips into the fire. Then they walk clockwise around the fire back to their seat, walking the circle of wholeness. I say, "Allow your voice when it wants to speak and your silence when it wants to be."

Closing and Benediction. We end by standing in a circle, and one by one, each person is invited to offer a one-word blessing before closing the circle. "May the thin place of this liminal time thin the spaces around your guarded heart to know you are surrounded by love."—*Valerie Luna Serrels*

AUTUMN BLESSING

> *May the lengthening shadows foretell new tales*
> *as the waning sun plays about the horizon,*
>
> *May the deep dark cradle of spring's promise glow warm*
> *in the deepening darkness of autumn nights,*
>
> *May the cold winds slow summer's vibrations,*
> *hushing them into folk songs and tales by the fire,*
>
> *May the blessing of the great mystery revealed in the changing seasons*
> *surround you and keep you warm,*
> *calm you and give you courage,*
> *connect you and give you community,*
> *comfort you and give you hope.*
> *—Mary Abma, Wild-Edge Offerings, Bright's Grove, ON*

WINTER'S SONG

On this darkest day
We hold on to the promise
Of lights lengthening
And embrace the quiet notes
Of winter's song.

—Mary Abma, Wild-Edge Offerings, Bright's Grove, ON

PRANYER FOR ADVENT

100

Divine Light,
Lover of the universe
Love incarnate
Love that is alive all over
our world today:
Warm our hearts and melt our indifference.
Ignite love within us that is big enough
to overcome our smallness, and
big enough to extend to all the earth
and all our more-than-human neighbors.
Luminous Love, shine deep within,
with a light that shares the darkness
with a graciousness that does not overpower.
May we, too,
be bearers of the Light.
Amen.

—Wendy Janzen, Burning Bush Forest Church,
Kitchener-Waterloo, ON

7
CONVERSATION WITH THE HOLY WILD
Solo Sauntering as Sermon

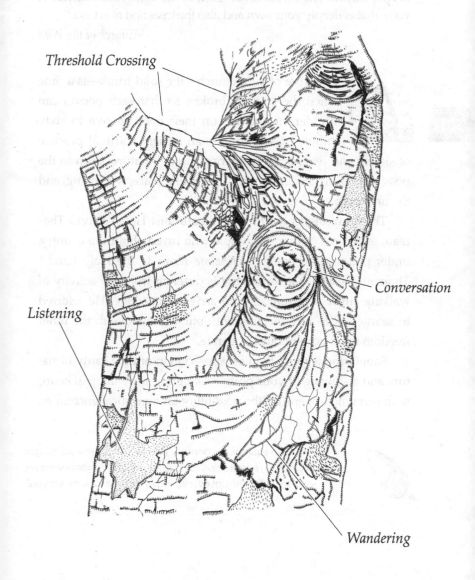

Threshold Crossing

Conversation

Listening

Wandering

"There is something about slowing down to be present in a wildish place for an extended time. First the silence allows you to hear your own voice beneath the chatter of distractions and to-do lists and self-evaluations. Then even that fades, and you can hear the voices of the wind and the rain and the chickadees. Eventually you can hear it: a deeper silence. The invitation to listen to the voice of the sacred. A voice that is deeply your own and also the trees and also God."

—*Church of the Wild*

 t the core of wild church—the solid trunk—is a time when the circle is broken so that each person can wander, or saunter, on their own for five to sixty minutes. Sauntering is an ancient spiritual practice of slowly and reverently wandering through nature, open to the possibility of an encounter with a particular place, wild being, and the unknown.

The term *saunter*, according to naturalist Henry David Thoreau, is derived "from idle people who roved about the country, under pretenses of going *a' la Sainte Terre*—to the Holy Land." Thoreau insisted that sauntering is different from the activity of walking either for exercise or to arrive somewhere. He referred to sauntering as reconnecting with our wildness, with the inner freedom to be led without an agenda.

Sauntering is more than an appreciation of the beauty of nature and a slowing of your pulse. Wandering with an open heart, with reverence, opens up the possibility for a mystical encounter.

 Before the saunter, tell people, "If you want to stay out longer than what we're agreeing to now, you must let someone know, or else we'll interrupt everything and come looking for you."

There is no need for special enlightenment training, nor is there expectation of some kind of deep spiritual insight. Rather, sauntering is a heart-opening practice that affirms that this ground where you live is, indeed, sacred. All land is holy land.

This time of solo wandering offers the true sermon of wild church. Participants receive messages particular to them, and they hear them from a variety of preachers: crow, moss, or unrelenting sun. The members of the natural world, all speaking in their unique leaf and wind and mushroom voices, pass on whispers of holy wisdom. This contemplative and yet playful form of spirituality has been practiced by monks and mystics throughout history. St. John of the Cross, a sixteenth-century mystic, recorded his practice of sauntering:

> *I was sad one day and went for a walk;*
> *I sat in a field.*
> *A rabbit noticed my condition and came near.*
> *It often does not take more than that to help at times—to just*
> *be close to creatures who are so full of knowing,*
> *so full of love that they don't—chat,*
> *they just gaze with their marvelous understanding.*

At a wild church gathering, everyone is invited to wander, regardless of experience, tradition, or mobility. Young children, in particular, seem to have an unquestioned connection with the spirit of a place. There is so much synergy between children and the natural world that they could easily lead us adults in appreciating, noticing, listening, and playing with the more-than-human world. We've even seen children and youths who have been domesticated by too many screens and technology come alive when offered the opportunity to slow down and relate to the natural world directly.

If your location is very wooded, you may need to set up a buddy system so people don't get lost. If there is cell service, share your number. Establish a safety protocol for sensitive terrain or poisonous plants, insects, or snakes.

SAUNTERING BEINGS

There is a secret language of nature. Learning to listen as wild ones speak is a practice of opening your imagination, clearing your mind of resistance, and letting your body remember. The land and all creatures speak in sacred whispers, and we have the capacity to connect, creature to creature, in a sacred conversation when we approach with reverence.

We have forgotten how to listen to the sacred voices in the wind and burning bushes. It is a spiritual practice that takes practice. It takes more than agreeing with a statement or acknowledging that all things come from stardust or placing an "Everything Is Sacred" bumper sticker on your car. We need to experience for ourselves the sacred presence that can be heard in the wilderness. The Hebrew term *Ba midbar* used throughout the Old Testament over three hundred times means "wilderness." But the primary meaning, according to the Hebrew-English lexicon, is "the organ which speaks." It also means "no words" or that which cannot be spoken in words. The land speaks to us still in voices that we can only hear when we are listening with reverence.

Mythologist Martin Shaw offers insight:

> *The new stories are like an echo-location arising from the Earth itself. In the living world, when certain animal calls collide with another being, they send an echo back to the caller, giving even an almost blind creature a sense of what is in their surrounding*

domain. I think the Earth has always done something similar.
It transmits pulses, coded information, lucid images, and then
sits back to see what echoes return from its messaging. When
the call hits whoever is tuned to receive it, it sends an echo back
to its source; it confirms relationship. It is very mysterious, and
requires a certain aliveness to pick it up.

This mysterious conversation is the soul of wild church.

STAGES OF SACRED SAUNTERING

There are no rules, and there is zero need to follow any particular pattern in sending people out to wander. In fact, trying to
explain these "stages" of sauntering can bring people back into
their heads and get in the way. But it is worth sharing here some
best practices of entering into sacred conversation during wild
church wanderings.

1. *Invitation.* An invitation is not a sermon. Nature is the preach-
    er, not you. The sermons come from lichen and scrub jays and
    empty creek beds. The role of the leader is to hold the space
    and invite your human congregants to leave the circle and
    connect with the preachers, teachers, and companions on the
    land. A theme, a quotation, or a story—even a focus on one

Solo sauntering can be a five-minute meditation where people
come back with one word to share, or it can be a full hour-long
immersion. Let people know the time and suggest ways for them
to return at the agreed-on time. You can send texts if there is
cell service or advise them to stay close enough to one other or
close enough to hear the drumming or bell (or loud hummingbird
or peacock calls!).

aspect of the value of sauntering—can serve as a focus as they wander. What happens on their saunter, though, often has nothing at all to do with your invitation. That's okay. Without an invitation, though, the container often feels too loose. As the leader, you'll probably want to stay close to the circle, holding the space as people head out to wander. Participants with mobility challenges can wander from their folding chairs under the tree without leaving the circle at all.

2. *Separation.* Invite your people to cross a threshold, which can be as simple as stepping over the edges of the circle, or perhaps they might watch for their own threshold: a path off the main trail or a tree branch creating an arc to cross under. Before crossing a threshold, take a moment to close your eyes, slow your breath, and make the stepping-over intentional. A prayer to open your imagination and release your expectations. You're stepping into the world as it actually is, which is enchanted and sacred.

3. *The Saunter.* Once you cross over the threshold, choose to approach everything with contemplative reverence. This is the core of the practice: simply walking with slowness, listening with tenderness, and pausing often. We practice paying attention so that we might cultivate our ability to hear the voice of the Sacred speaking to us through all that is. Allow yourself to be drawn to something (the river, the sun, shadows, the breeze) or someone (a cloud, a hawk, a bug, a tree) that seems to be calling you. Don't question or second-guess. Feeling drawn to a particular place isn't something you can force. It requires some degree of letting go of your monkey mind and listening from that deeper place of knowing.

4. *Permission.* Once a particular other (a place or being) summons you, approach them with reverence. Conversation is a

two-way relationship, and you don't approach another person to "experience" them. When you want to meet someone new, you begin with a request to join them. After all, each being has their own concerns, relationships, and priorities. If you feel a yes, settle down in your chair or on the ground or lie down on your back. Simply *be present*. Wait. Resist the temptation to fill the blank space with your own voice and just allow the silence to rise up.

5. *Conversation.* As you settle down in this place that has chosen you, remember that you aren't there to figure out why—at least not with your strategic mind. You are there to listen with humility and vulnerability. Listen to the echoes of birds, the flowing of water, or the interaction between the wind and the leaves. Even the human sounds of machines and dogs barking are a reminder that humans are part of this place. Let the sounds become a gateway to a deeper sense of connection and presence. Take the time to observe the details of the natural world around you. Notice with all your senses the patterns, shapes, colors, and movements of plants, animals, and the landscape. Once you experience a sense of the other as a sacred being, authentic conversation can happen. Conversation is not chatting—it's deeper than that. It's entering into someone else's world and allowing their stories to break your heart open.

All beings, including plants, animals, and natural elements, possess their unique ways of communicating. To think

Invite those who have mobility limitations to stay settled under your tree, within your circle. They can get just as much out of sitting still and listening to the tree above you as anyone wandering to the top of a hill.

we can know what a tree is feeling might sound like anthropomorphic arrogance. But to think we actually know what our child or our partner is feeling is a form of arrogance as well. Listening deeply, without pretending we know what they're saying, paradoxically opens us to hearing. It helps to begin with a genuine appreciation of what you notice about this other, paying attention to what is uniquely special about them. Imagine, with empathic kindness, what it might feel like to be them. Notice the relationships important to them. You may be the only human who has noticed and paid appreciative attention to this particular lizard or bend in the river. Like a dog or a child who brightens up with your full attention, so do all living beings. Feel your way into the reciprocity of the encounter. Can you feel a sense of gratitude for the particularity of your attention?

Sitting with this more-than-human other, notice which feelings and memories or images arise in you. Contemplate the mystery of your connection with them and how their qualities might touch you. What is evoked in you? You may want to make notes in the form of poetry or journaling or sketching or a song arising from within your body. Or simply listen deeply, allowing images and emotions to visit you. With curiosity, ask if there is anything from this encounter that might speak to your own life and journey.

Try not to create expectations of some kind of astounding experience every time you wander. It is enough to observe the calls of the birds as citizens of this place. But when you listen long enough and with respect and reverence, you may just be surprised by what you hear in response.

6. *Gratitude and Return.* When it is time to return, as in any relationship, authentic gratitude is in order. Indigenous peoples often leave gifts of tobacco for the water or the land as

gratitude and blessing. Your gift could simply be a poem, a song, a smile, or a respectful bow. Your tears may be the gift. Your full attention is also a gift.

You may want to ask your place or being if there is something to bring back to the altar that symbolizes your encounter: a stone, a rusty tin can, a pine cone. But wait for an answer. We need to be careful about treating others not as objects of our own devotion but as independent beings in and of themselves.

When you return, cross over the same threshold again. Turn and offer gratitude one more time for this enchanted encounter. Return prepared to share your experience in the circle.

STORIES & PRACTICES

A SACRED CONVERSATION WITH AN OAK TREE. At one recent Church of the Wild service, during our wandering time, I was drawn to a particular oak tree, its roots spread out in all directions at the base of the trunk before descending into the soil. I sat on the ground with my back against this tree, my legs jutting out like the oak's roots.

After sitting for a while, I felt called to stand up, move to another point on the trunk, and face the tree; I closed my eyes, hugging the oak, pressing my chest against the bark. Looking out, I found myself reflecting on how this tree "lived here," how it was never bored being in this place, and then I imagined the oak "seeing" in all directions, whereas I am limited with eyes only in the front of my head. Here, I sensed an interesting rebuttal. It seemed as if the tree was saying, "No, you're not limited only to what you can see before your eyes. You humans also have the ability to 'see' with 360-degree sight."

I don't want to be too quick in "explaining away" my communion with the oak; I want to allow that part about 360 degrees of seeing among humans to work within me for a while. I'm still pondering and unpacking the layers of what it might mean. I do understand that I value this relational ideal of entering into "conversations" with a particular beetle, a specific rock, a unique bend in the creek, or, on this day, that special oak tree. I appreciate this invitation into one-on-one connection. It seems to be where the magic happens.—*Michael Malley, Sacred Ground Wild Church & Sangha, Columbus, OH*

PAYING EXQUISITE ATTENTION. One time, during a wandering, we were practicing the gift of slowing down. I was paying intense attention to a particular very small pearl crescent butterfly. I watched her wander from leaf to leaf, and then I witnessed the butterfly closing her tiny eyes and breathing slowly and evenly, taking a wee nap in the afternoon. This experience shifted my consciousness.—*Mary Abma, Wild-Edge Offerings, Bright's Grove, ON*

FLIRTATIOUS WANDER. As you walk the path, in life and out on the land, pay exquisite attention to what is happening at the margin of your awareness, on the edges of things. Soft signals from Mystery. Small wonders. Flickering signals. What is wanting to "flirt" with you? If something catches your eye, behold it for a little while. What's happening? Then you might close your eyes. Notice how your body is responding. Is there some physical sensation? Some movement that is happening or wants to happen in your body or some sound you want to make? When this feels complete, open your eyes, offer a gesture of gratitude, and move on. What else wants to catch your eye today?—*Jim Hall, Wild Earth Spiritual Community, Washington, DC*

MESSAGE FROM WATER. In one wild church service, I felt drawn to the water. I listened and felt that the water said, "Return. Return to me. To the depths of your true nature. Return to the slow eddies and turbulent currents, to undulating rhythms, to flowing blood, lymph, sweat, tears. To cells suspended, caressed and hydrated. Mingling in a wave-pulsed matrix. To the briny, buoyant womb, while the moon whispers invitations to advance and recede and reflect."—*Tamara Grenier, Lowcountry Wild Church, Charleston, SC*

CREATIVE INTERACTIVE WANDERINGS. We play with offering some interactive, different kinds of wanderings, depending on where we gather. We might be just lying on the ground and noticing the sky. One time, my coleader, who is an artist, brought out an easel with pastels and invited people to add things to it over the wandering time. My favorite experience was when he set up a big mirror in the woods. The reflection of your face and the woods looking at you was powerful and led to a lot of insights in our sharing time. You don't need these extra things, but I like that it helps expand our imaginations and experiences.—*Kathy Escobar, Forest Church, Golden, CO*

SAUNTERING STATIONS. Occasionally, we do our wanderings a little bit differently. Once we did a solstice offering focused on walking in darkness to light. I set up little stations—one by a small pond, another by a larger pond, another a little bit deeper into the woods—and invited people to go to each of these stations. They began carrying a small bucket of compost, and when they went to the small pond and spent time there walking or resting, they then released some of the compost into the water that symbolized those things that no longer serve them in their lives. At the next station, they were given four flowers, and they were invited to gather in mind, body, and emotions around what they were grateful for over the past year. At the third station, they were given four seeds and spent time in that space with an openness to what they were being called to, to what is being seeded in their lives.

We gathered back in our circle for a fire ceremony following the wandering and had time to share about their experiences and offer two flowers and seeds to the fire.—*Greg Turk, Wild Sacred, Seattle, WA*

A FEW IDEAS FOR WANDERS.

113

Ephemeral Mandalas. Wherever you are drawn, settle there for a little while, listening. Then begin to create a mandala circle with the stones, twigs, leaves, and other little pieces of life in your place. Treat it as a contemplative practice, not to try to create any kind of spiritual moment but to clear your mind. Immerse yourself like a child in the making of art in gratitude for the beauty of this place. Bless it with love before returning.

Attentive Praise Wander. Offer your full attention to any particular being in your sauntering. Simply notice their natural authenticity. They are purely and fully what they are without self-consciousness, without any apparent wish to be otherwise, without even a glimmer of identity crisis. Look at them carefully, listen to them, and touch them (if possible and not harmful to them). Wonder about their unique and astonishing ways and about how they manage to be themselves so fully and genuinely. And then notice within yourself where you are also authentic and speak out loud until your voice feels most genuinely like you (as opposed to someone trying to be nice, strong, bold).

Mirroring Wander. Once you arrive at your contemplative place, observe closely this other who has called you. Stand up and move or dance or chant in a way that mirrors them. Wonder: How might they be mirroring you?—*Victoria Loorz*

THE WEE ONES GET IT. At one gathering, a mom joined us for the first time with her four-year-old daughter, who listened carefully during the first part of our service. During the wandering, the invitation was simply to greet the beings with love. The little one knew exactly what to do. She very seriously and quietly walked up to every tree and bush around our circle and shook hands with the low branches, hugged the bushes, and kissed the flowers. When we returned to share our stories, she was the first to walk into the center of the circle, holding something lightly in her closed hands. She said, "The trees gave me a gift" and gently laid down a pine cone onto our little altar of stones and flowers.—*Victoria Loorz*

YOUTHS ENGAGE EASILY. We don't program anything separate for children. We encourage them to be curious and playful and to engage and participate at their own level. Mostly, they explore and have fun. One time, a tween girl came with her mother. During the wander, they went together, observing and paying attention to the trees, sky, water, etc. When they returned, the daughter shared, "Everything was so beautiful! Imagine how beautiful God is!" The mother shared how grateful she was for the opportunity to see the world through her daughter's eyes and to talk about God together. One time, I led a group of teen girls on a wild beauty walk. It was a great experience, inviting them to find something that drew their attention, observe what made it beautiful, and reflect on how it mirrored their own beauty. They loved it!—*Wendy Janzen, Burning Bush Forest Church, Kitchener-Waterloo, ON*

FREE PLAY AND NATURE PROJECTS FOR KIDS. Free play and exploration are our base for children and teens. From this foundation, we can facilitate group actions that engage and unite children. Some of our favorite planned activities with children include making fairy houses from materials in nature; foraging for berries and other edibles (with a knowledgeable adult); making art and jewelry out of found natural objects; cleaning up trash; mindfully eating outside; identifying trees; going on nature treasure hunts; drawing, writing, and reading in the outdoors.—*Heather Wolfe, Wild Church Taftsville Chapel, Woodstock, VT*

INTERGENERATIONAL WANDERING. It's wandering time during a wild church gathering. Looking around the park, I see three people leaning against friendly trees, one woman lying on the grass looking up at the clouds, and another sitting five feet away from a tall grass bush swaying in the breezy heat. One of our elderly participants has chosen to stay in her lawn chair under the tree in our circle. She sits with her eyes closed, listening with ease to hummingbird poetry she will share with us soon. Two young boys are running down the hill, chasing one another, as their mother gains an unusual respite of solitude. Nobody tells them to slow down. A preschool girl is building a "fairy house," she says, out of twigs with her cousin. I can see down by the shaded creek that several people took off their shoes to cross to the other side, and they are scattered along the edges, dipping their feet in the water, sitting on rocks with their journals, and watching tiny waterfalls carry leaves downstream. It's early summer, and who knows how long this seasonal creek will last.—*Victoria Loorz*

DANDELION TEA. During the wandering and wondering portion of our gathering, I accompany the kids in their own contemplative wandering so parents can have their own solo experience. In May, we picked dandelions to make flower blossom tea, leaf tea, and root coffee that we served after the service.—*Heather Wolfe, Wild Church Taftsville Chapel, Woodstock, VT*

LEARN FROM THE YOUNGEST MEMBERS. It was wonderful to witness a baby in our wild church carefully observe the interactions of the adults, especially the singing, drumming, and rattling. She explored a pine cone from all angles, investigated a leaf, and followed an insect intently. The eight- to ten-year-old children are most active in sharing after wandering, bringing insightful awareness to issues of sustainability and conservation. They say things like "I was careful not to step on the moss too much because I didn't want to damage it" and "I think the trees are saying they don't want to be cut down anymore, and they are home to so many creatures."—*Tamara Grenier, Lowcountry Wild Church, Charleston / Johns Island, SC*

8

RE-STORYING OUR PLACE
Sharing in Circle

Witnessing One Another

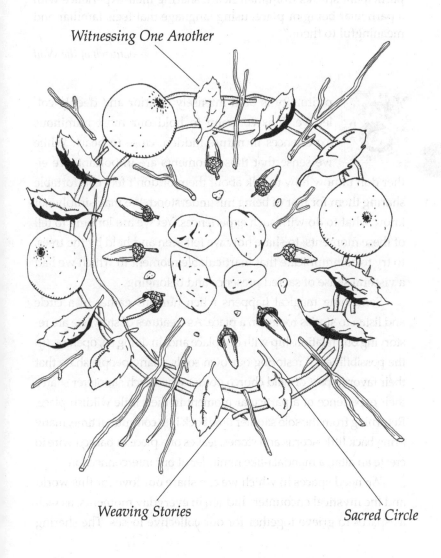

Weaving Stories

Sacred Circle

"They wander back one by one with their stories from the land. . . . We've been listening to the preaching of the creek and the cricket and now we have an opportunity to share our experiences. There is no hierarchy. Everyone speaks out of their experience, where they wandered, what happened, what they thought about. . . .each participant speaks from their heart, sharing their experience with a particular being or place, using language that feels familiar and meaningful to them."

—*Church of the Wild*

pirituality is both intensely interior and deeply collective. It is common to hold our most numinous experiences in nature hidden, close to heart. While we sense that those moments are important, we either don't know how to talk about them or don't feel comfortable sharing them for fear of being misunderstood. We may simply not know what to do with such experiences. Yet we are longing to tell of these moments: to share how we felt seen and held by the trees, to try to communicate that inarticulable moment in which we had a visceral sense of sacred presence and belonging.

Something magical happens when humans gather in a circle and listen to stories rooted in a place. As creatures of story, we are re-storying our relationship with our place and, in doing so, opening up the possibilities of restoring our own souls. Many people share that their favorite part of wild church occurs when each saunterer shares their experience of a particular moment in their little wildish place. Returning from the solo saunter time back into communal time, many bring back little acorns and stones, leaves or a piece of barbed wire to create an altar, a mandala-like reminder of our interconnection.

We need spaces in which we can share our love for this world and the mystical encounters hidden in everyday moments, as well as spaces to grieve together for our collective losses. The sharing

Sometimes people will bring back a leaf or a twig or a bit of barbed wire from their wander and offer it to the altar in the middle of the circle. If they've asked permission, we can see this practice as a way to honor the experience and the particular beings we've encountered.

after wandering in wild church is a place of safety to speak without judgment about what we may not be able to utter anywhere else.

GRACIOUSNESS

After wandering and regrouping in a circle, each participant is invited to share their experience. Some return with profound realizations, others with simple stories of stillness. For example, someone may share an appreciation for a fallen log with whom they sat—a log who may be a mother tree nourishing others in the forest for as long as she did while she was "alive"; this might spur a conversation later about the real meaning of aliveness. This kind of shared storytelling flattens any hierarchy of wisdom. Wisdom is accessible not only from the trees, wind, and grasshoppers; it flows through each of us.

There is no advice-giving and no correcting. There is no validating certain stories and condemning others. It doesn't matter whether a member of the circle uses the words *God* or *Jesus* or words like *Goddess* and *Energy* or says simple things like "it was so pretty" because they are sharing from their heart. Leaders and listeners model compassionate, nonjudgmental, deep listening. Every experience is honored, and together the circle engages in collective meaning-making. As leaders hold the space for conversation within a safe container, group members open their hearts, feel seen, and trust their own experience without feeling like they're "doing it wrong." Authentic conversations allow us to draw closer to the other while getting to know ourselves more deeply.

Ojibwe Canadian author and journalist Richard Wagamese captures the value of sharing in circles, a practice of humans throughout history. "Sometimes people just need to talk. They need to be heard," he writes. "They need the validation of my time, my silence, my unspoken compassion. They don't need advice, or sympathy, or counseling. They need to hear the sound of their own voices speaking their own truths, articulating their own feelings, as those may be at a particular moment."

As the group listens with generosity to one another, each story becomes larger, inviting us to hold these encounters as sacred. We are not meant to figure them out but to simply receive them as we would a meaningful dream or synchronistic occurrence. You will find that the stories from the others in the circle open up your own experience, often interweaving in mysterious ways.

LISTENING AS SPIRITUAL PRACTICE

While sauntering, we are remembering how to listen to the wind and stars and rivers. Perhaps you have entered into a wordless conversation with a rabbit who stopped to look you straight in the eye. But it is during the time of sharing that a sense of *something sacred* emerges as the simple stories are shared.

Many people don't think they have much of a story to tell. But an observation from someone else's sharing in the circle might

When the groups are too large to hear stories from everyone, you can form groups of two or three, which can be less intimidating for newcomers. After a few minutes of sharing in small groups, return to the large circle, where everyone has the option to offer five words to highlight their experience. This is done "popcorn style," so no one is ever pressured to share. The results are often poignant, sometimes funny, and usually poetic.

The facilitator's role is to listen deeply to what is being shared and to hold the space with compassion and respect. Pay attention to the energy that is present and be attuned to any emotions or tensions that arise. Offer support and validation to participants and encourage them to be present with their own feelings and experiences.

break open a deeper meaning. There may be no objective meaning in your encounter with a shy spider weaving a luminous web, but there can be a significant subjective meaning. Sharing the experience helps us regard it as something meaningful, even if we never "figure out" the meaning. Often, a coherent thread emerges from the stories shared within a group. The stories weave together to tell an even larger story. We are re-storying our place. Sometimes meaning is illuminated only when these intimate sacred experiences are told together.

This wisdom from wild church leader Michael Malley leads us into the shared stories and wisdom from many others that follow:

> *Compassionate listening in our Wild Church sharing circles is not just a means to an end; it is an end in itself. Listening with kindness and a desire to simply understand (without correcting or improving upon what the other says) is something of a lost art in modernity. We must begin to develop this skill set once again. Encouraging others to describe their solo nature experiences through their own religious, spiritual, or secular languages, we broaden our understanding of both the natural world and each other. Listening with curiosity, allowing people space to share about their sacred wanderings in their unique ways, we grow and learn.*

STORIES & PRACTICES

HOLDING THE SPACE. *The following is a list of best practices for holding space in your sharing circle. These ideas and practices are collected from several wild church leaders.*

Set the Intention and Guidelines. Begin by orienting people to the time of sharing. Witnessing one another's stories deepens the experience and often reveals meaning. Encourage participants to bring an open and curious mindset and to respect each other's perspectives and experiences. Every week, remind them to share their experiences, using "I" statements rather than preaching or showing how much they know about a topic. Establish natural guidelines that promote respectful communication and active listening.

Use a Talking Piece. Consider using a talking piece, such as a small stick or large stone, that is passed around the circle. The person holding the talking piece is the only one who speaks, and everyone else listens attentively. This helps promote active listening and ensure that everyone has an opportunity to share. Anyone is welcome to simply pass the talking piece if they are not ready to share. Come back to them later and check in to see if they'd like to share before closing the circle.

Share Your Name. It is good practice to invite each speaker to share their name before sharing, even if everyone already knows each other. This ritual habit is beneficial in the long run. As new people show up on other occasions, they will hear each participant's name before they share. This practice nurtures an open, welcoming space rather than creating a closed circle of friends that new participants must "push through" to enter.

Offer Mirroring. While it is good practice to encourage no cross talk, there are times when the leader and other participants can affirm and connect with an individual's or the group's experience. A few words of affirmation or reflection of the essence of their sharing can help each member feel included and important. We know who we are by how we are mirrored. When someone truly sees and mirrors us, we tend to more readily receive and integrate our own experience.

Sacred Silence before Speaking. Invite a moment of sacred silence after each sharing. Many of us wait for another person to stop talking just so we can start! But we hope to nurture deep listening during our solo time in the natural world, and we want to do the same within the sharing circle. A quiet moment after each sharing honors both the speaker and what they have contributed to the community.

Sensitivity to Emotions. Time alone in nature sometimes opens our awareness to wounds—in ourselves, in society, and in the Earth herself. People sometimes share from deep places during Church of the Wild sharing circles. Our goal is to be sensitive and compassionate listeners. When someone comes with deep emotions, others can get uncomfortable. It is up to the leader to hold that space to allow for emotions without trying to fix or even comfort. The compassionate practice of witnessing one another's strong emotions, without reacting, is a forgotten gift.

Close the Sharing Time. Take a moment to thank everyone for their participation and acknowledge the insights and wisdom that were shared.—*Michael Malley of Sacred Ground; Leah Rampy of Church of the Wild ~ Two Rivers; Melissa Fritchle, a guide at Seminary of the Wild Earth; and Victoria Loorz*

· **OPEN TO ALL.** As leaders or facilitators of a spiritually diverse group, we know it is incumbent on us to create a space where everyone may be heard and appreciated. Our church/sangha includes people identifying themselves as Christian, Buddhist, or some other religious tradition, spiritual but not religious, humanist, pagan, agnostic, or atheist. Whatever the speaker's beliefs or frame of reference, our aspiration is to give them a safe place to share.—*Michael Malley, Sacred Ground Community Church & Sangha, Columbus, OH*

124

MEANING-MAKING. In Gathering Ground, we welcome all paths of meaning-making, knowing the mystery of meaning goes by many names. We welcome them all. Leaders are careful about using words like *Spirit, God,* or *soul.* If they are used, we use other synonyms also to keep the space welcoming for those who eschew that framing. *Meaning-making* is the agreed-upon term for what we do. At the same time, we do try to set up participants to be respectful of the words that others might use for Mystery.—*Beth Amsbary, Gathering Ground, Seattle, WA*

UNEXPECTED SACRED CONNECTIONS. During one of my favorite services, after wandering, a man shared about trying to grow strawberries in his garden space and feeling frustrated with the slow progress of the plants. He tried all the gardening tricks, from soil amendments to pest control, and finally resorted to speaking lovingly and praying over the strawberry plants. One day while working in the garden, he softly spoke to the plants and offered a prayer, and then, lifting one of the leaves, he discovered a large, ripe strawberry. He had been hesitant to see the sacred connection until his wandering.—*Tamara Grenier, Lowcountry Wild Church, Charleston, SC*

RIVER SPEAKS. During one service, everyone drew a famous quotation about rivers from a basket. Each person walked down to the Juniata River and stood or sat by the riverbank to meditate on the specific quote they had chosen. When the group reconvened, it was wonderful seeing both the similarities and differences of each person's connection to the river and their chosen quote.— *Dana Jefferson, Allegheny Cathedral of the Wild, Huntingdon, PA*

125

BEST UNDERSTOOD OUTDOORS. After the readings and our solo wandering time, one of our members, Jeff, came back and spoke of how he walked in a direction where he thought a stream would be, even though he could not see it from where he had started. Jeff said it reminded him of the fruitless fig tree: things often exist unseen, gurgling and bubbling just beyond our current vision. He said fresh fruits are "growing within us," even though it may not yet be time for them to ripen and be seen; another year of nurturance may be required before the fruit will manifest. —*Michael Malley, Sacred Ground Wild Church & Sangha, Columbus, OH*

THE VALUE OF SHARING STORIES. I was leading an eco-spirituality retreat with a group of religious and deeply spiritual people. They were also dedicated climate activists engaged in climate work, and they came from a dozen different churches in the Portland, Oregon, area. I asked the members of the group to share a story with the person sitting next to them about an encounter or a place or a moment in nature where they experienced a sense of the numinous.

Afterward, in the larger circle, a man in his early eighties told of a transformational encounter with a moose he'd experienced in his thirties. It opened his eyes, he said, to holiness in the form of this magnificent (and huge!) creature. He felt connected. He shared how that encounter changed the direction of his life and ignited his lifelong involvement in environmental causes. He had never named it as something sacred before. He had never made the connection between this experience and his actual spirituality, only his vocation. His wife of nearly fifty years shared with awe that she had never heard this pivotal story.—*Victoria Loorz*

CIRCLE COMMITMENTS. *Here is a sample circle commitment that could be read at the beginning of this time.* To honor one another and our wildest, truest selves, we commit to: *Witness* each person with respect and reverence. Imagine a small circle of silence around you as you listen deeply with your heart. Resist distraction or thinking ahead to what you will say. *Speak* your truth from the heart. Take a few deep breaths and allow silence to gather your thoughts. Ask yourself, "What is the essence, the heart of what I want to share?" Be mindful of the time so that all others have time to share. *Respond* sparingly as friends share to let them know they've been heard and their stories are valued. A simple nod or bow or "thank you" is often enough to affirm each person's sharing. Actively resist temptation to judge, offer your insights or advice, or even comfort. *Confidentiality* is essential so that people feel safe sharing at deeper levels.—*Victoria Loorz*

LISTENING AGREEMENTS. The Journey Center has a long practice of creating sacred space with listening agreements. Two of my favorites are trusting the work of the Spirit in others and keeping our sharing in "I" language. By describing ourselves as Christ centered, it also lets those who may not identify with a religion know that they may hear some Christ language, without requiring them to do so themselves.—*Mindy Braun, Wild Journeys, Santa Rosa, CA*

COLLECTIVE AGREEMENTS. The majority of our folk intentionally avoid affiliating with organized religion. We've evolved four agreements for how we are together, shared at the beginning of every meeting and every gathering. This helps us create an intentional space for everyone to join. We read each agreement slowly. And we often encourage a physical response to affirm our agreement, such as putting our hands on our hearts or a playful thumbs-up with a hearty "oh yeah!"

> *We take care of ourselves (physical and heart needs).*
>
> *We listen for each person. Simply listening and witnessing is a valuable way to participate. We are grateful for pauses and silence.*
>
> *We share from our own experience. As listeners, we contribute to brave space by asking permission before commenting or asking questions.*
>
> *We welcome all paths of meaning-making, knowing the mystery of meaning goes by many names. We welcome them all.*
>
> —*Beth Amsbury, Gathering Ground, Seattle, WA*

9
OFFERINGS AND BENEDICTION
Practicing Wild Reciprocity

Transformation

Restoration

Service to Earth

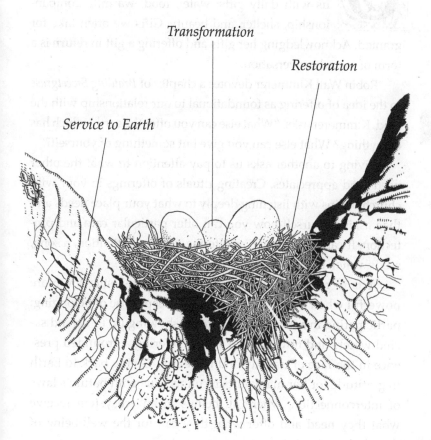

"The time has come to lift that veil of fog and return to intimate relationship with the living world. More and more of us are taking our place, once again, as full participants in the web of life, which we remember is held together by love."

—*Church of the Wild*

fferings are gifts of gratitude best understood as a form of sacred reciprocity. Earth herself presents us with daily gifts: water, food, warmth, companionship, shelter, and beauty. Gifts we often take for granted. Acknowledging her gifts and offering a gift in return is a form of sacred conversation.

Robin Wall Kimmerer devotes a chapter of *Braiding Sweetgrass* to the idea of offering as foundational to our relationship with the land. Kimmerer asks, "What else can you offer the earth, which has everything? What else can you give but something of yourself?"

Giving to another asks us to pay attention to what the other needs and appreciates. Creating rituals of offerings in your wild church begins with listening deeply to what your place needs and then asking yourself how you can offer particular care and protection. It can be as simple as offering your full attention, a song, seeds, water, or art as an act of beauty.

Acts of restoration, conservation, and eco-justice are more powerful when they are offered from a deep sense of belonging: participating in a community garden, showing up to defend sacred waters and forests, even simply offering a grounded presence in the face of tragedy and upheaval. Giving back to Earth in gratitude for her many gifts reconnects us with nature's laws of interconnection, where all beings in an ecosystem receive what they need and offer what they can for the well-being of the whole.

CARRYING THE WISDOM OF THE WILD BACK HOME

Benediction means "blessing," a religious word that marks the end of a church service. Essentially the message is "go in peace." It's a blessing with encouragement to take the peace of God you've experienced inside the church and bring it "out there" into the world.

At the close of a wild church gathering, the blessings are similar but reversed: take the peace you've been experiencing "out there" in the wild and bring it back into your life inside the village, like the return home of the old hero's journey. The insights and wisdom gleaned from your experience reconnecting with the Sacred in your place compel you to do something about it. To live differently.

WITHIN OURSELVES

Wild church isn't just a gathering. It's a way of life. We carry the wild church ethos—of relationality, love, awareness, and opening to *what is* in each moment—back to our day-to-day lives. We can ask ourselves: How does my daily life resemble the reverent approach of a contemplative sauntering? Am I fully embodied in my engagement with other humans, more-than-humans, and places? If we integrate a wild church approach into our daily practice and orientation to the world, our lives become a continuous benediction.

Just like at a gathering, we can begin any day by grounding ourselves in our bodies and making conscious connection with the Earth. We can, even briefly, listen to the crows with reverence or approach spiders with curiosity rather than fear. We can look up at night and remember with awe that we belong to a communion of interconnected life that includes even the stars.

Opening ourselves to the sacred wild, simply by going out and listening and being present, changes our relationship with

131

Earth and with other humans. And that practice changes our sense of who we are. Moving from old story to new is not an erasure or a conquering; it is a gentle surrender to the wisdom of the Earth, of the oak, of our souls. This is wild church.

A BENEDICTION

> *May the Spirit of the Abundant Earth*
> *Awaken you to live in the knowledge that*
> *You are of the earth, from the earth, and returning to the earth.*
>
> *May the Tree of life*
> *Rise up in you,*
> *Root you deeply into the ground*
> *And nourish you to extend your branches out into the world*
>
> *Blessings of the Earth,*
> *Of the great conversation that holds all things together*
> *Be upon you with boundless gratitude.*
> *Amen.*

STORIES &
PRACTICES

WORKING WITH COMMUNITY PARTNERSHIPS. One of the ways we are deepening our relationship with the lower Fraser watershed is by restoring wildlife habitat through partnerships with local churches. A few years ago, we started working with a church in North Vancouver to replace invasives with native plants along a salmon stream on their grounds. And now the project has grown to partnerships with ten congregations in the region to create small pollinator gardens or native medicinal gardens. We have partnered with another church to take part in Canada's Two Billion Trees program, planting a mini-forest on what used to be a church lawn. Our partnerships with church communities help us make a more significant impact on our restoration efforts and also the church communities grow a sense of their connection and care outside the doors of their building.—*Laurel Dykstra, Salal + Cedar, Vancouver, BC*

PARTICIPATING IN COMMUNITY ACTIVISM. We participated in a statewide movement of religious and other organizations in a campaign called 1000 flags / 1000 waters to "empower and unite frontline communities and water protectors engaged in resistance" against the Mountain Valley and Atlantic Coast Pipelines threatening forests and water sources in Virginia. Blue precut flags were mailed out to participant communities and organizations. We drew symbols and words on our flag in solidarity with frontline communities and ceremonially "baptized" our flag in the waters of the creek where we gather, with blessings and prayers for clean waters everywhere.—*Valerie Luna Serrels, Shenandoah Valley Church of the Wild, Harrisonburg, VA*

TREE PLANTING. We took part in a collaborative tree-planting project with the Interfaith Water Stewards II and the Cedar Tree Institute. Together, we planted five hundred northern white cedar trees in the Yellow Dog Community Forest. Part of our orientation to the day included an overview of forestry practices and the vital role that cedar trees play in the tradition of the Anishinabe peoples of our region.—*Lanni Lantto, U.P. Wild Church, Marquette, MI*

ADVOCACY FOR OUR NEIGHBORS. We rotate sites for our gatherings. One place we meet is a wetland site being threatened by development. Our relationship with this place has led some members to speak up at public hearings about the proposed development. Others from our community contributed to an art show on behalf of a coalition to save these same wetlands. Our discussion of planting native plants has led to members reworking their own gardens.—*Dana Jefferson, Allegheny Cathedral of the Wild, Huntingdon, PA*

SUPPORT FOR ENDANGERED FRIENDS. As an offering to the endangered species in our region, we created an Advent ritual of "adopting" a particular animal. We researched local endangered animals and created fifteen packets of information on each species.

For a five-dollar donation per packet, families can "adopt" a particular animal and commit to praying for them through the upcoming year. In remembering them, we also look for ways to support saving those on the critically endangered list. Our community has also made wooden crosses to put up along the streets in the Upper Peninsula in remembrance of the lost creatures as well as animal friends (our fellows) who have already gone extinct.—*Lanni Lantto, U.P. Wild Church, Marquette, MI*

CREATIVE RESTORATION IN ACTION. In lieu of traditional offerings, we have been doing action-oriented offerings that give back to creation. Here are a few we have done in our wild church: an Epiphany blessing of our Earth home, a bee hotel we created for hospitality to our pollinator neighbors, placing ashes ceremonially under lilacs, planting a tree and seeds and a peace pole. We spread wildflower seeds in a patch of empty dirt. Spreading compost is an offering, as are our tears and petitions. We regularly cook a community soup to donate to the local food shelf.—*Heather Wolfe, Wild Church Taftsville Chapel, Woodstock, VT*

SUPPORTING COMMUNITY RESTORATION. When we talk about offerings, we make it a regular habit to ask participants about eco-spiritual projects of reciprocity happening close to their homes and hearts. And then we'll include those in our newsletters and announcements, encouraging one another to attend what feels right while also paying attention and tending to their own particular biosphere. For example, one of our participants began a Weed Warrior project in conjunction with the Maryland National Park

135

and Planning Commission. His Tree Friends group is cutting English ivy, kudzu, and other invasive plants that are choking trees in the large park near his home. Another participant is often away clearing trails in various national parks. Others inform us of their native gardens and keep us on our toes identifying and seasonally observing native species where we gather.—*Sarah Anders, Wild Earth Spiritual Community, Washington, DC*

FISH BLESSINGS. In April, we had a special outing. Our whole wild church community gathered at a brook in our town to watch the alewife fish attempt to swim up a fish ladder to make their way to the ocean. The children helped gather pine cones and pine needles and arrange them to create a big heart near the brook. Then they sent blessings to the fish.—*Diane Anderson, Chapel in the Pines, Wellesley, MA*

TREE BLESSINGS. One way to support local tree-planting efforts as a wild church is to talk with the organizers of volunteer tree-planting efforts (such as Tree People, Arbor Day, local county or city efforts) to see if you could offer a suggestion for a simple, nonsectarian spiritual practice that the volunteers can do while planting the trees. Ask people to bless the tree before planting them: "Little sapling, I offer you many wild blessings to grow and find all the nutrients you need, to be strong and grow deep." This practice can establish a personal relationship with a particular tree, inviting people to go back to visit "their" tree.—*Victoria Loorz*

PLANTING A GARDEN. We meet on private land with gardens and space to wander. One year, we created a circle-shaped three sisters garden (corn, beans, squash) next to where we gather. We learned about these gardens through Robin Wall Kimmerer's *Braiding Sweetgrass*. We later added a circle of stumps in the center of the garden, which is where our kids gather. We hold a planting ceremony in the spring when we plant and a harvest celebration in the fall that includes making soup with the three sisters. During Advent season, we transform the circle into a spiral lined with luminaries. It is a sacred space.—*Heather Wolfe, Wild Church Taftsville Chapel, Woodstock, VT*

Listening is at the heart of the wild church: listening to your soul, listening to the Earth, listening deeply to the Spirit, and listening to your community. Are you being called to create a wild church gathering? The questions below will help you listen. Set apart some time to reflect and take some notes on your wild wonderings. To do this, we recommend that you saunter contemplatively through different places in your region that might be calling you. Bring a little chair and a pen, along with this book and a journal or notebook (or just write here in the book—whatever works best for you). As you take notes, hold the emerging vision growing within you. Listen. Approach with reverence as you ask yourself these questions. Resist overthinking. Trust your immediate answers; you can research and think about it more later. See what emerges as you let your place know that you long to enter into sacred relationship.

LISTENING TO YOUR SOUL

You may not see yourself as a spiritual leader. But something has called you to draw people into deeper relationship with the Sacred and the Earth. There are many ways to step into this call. A wild church is one path that people take because they need an expression of church that aligns with their rewilding spirituality. You may be surprised how many others in your community are waiting to join you.

VISION: Jot a few notes about the vision for starting a wild church in your region. What is blooming within you?

MOTIVATIONS: Why are you doing this? What is motivating you to consider starting a wild church gathering? Consider what and who is calling you.

VALUES: What are your core values? Do they align with emerging values in the movement: sacred presence in all things, kindred interconnection and belonging, conversation?

SPIRITUAL OR ANCESTRAL HERITAGE: What is your spiritual tradition? What is the spiritual story of your ancestors? Where do you most experience spiritual connection? While people from many different traditions and beliefs will attend your gathering, you don't want to try to be everything to everyone. Be you. And invite everyone else to be themselves.

UNIQUE GIFTS: We are called to lead out of our unique gifts, experiences, interests, and even our woundings. What really brings you alive? What do you uniquely bring to the gathering?

FEARS. Fears are normal emotions when stepping into something new, particularly something that challenges the status quo. Naming your fears helps to befriend them, to thank them for trying to protect you. Recognize, though, that while these fears are trying to keep you safe, they're also keeping you small. This work requires us to step fully into our whole, large, remarkable selves in service to Earth and Spirit.

MEASURING SUCCESS: By what metrics will you measure your success? Numbers of people who show up? The ways people engage in conservation, eco-justice, or social justice actions? Or something more difficult to measure like softened hearts and transformed worldviews?

NEEDS: What questions are arising for you? What would you need to move forward with this vision? Who do you need to talk with? What are the next steps? Make notes about your questions and ideas.

TITLE: You may not be comfortable calling yourself a "wild church pastor" in any way. And that's okay. You can call yourself what feels right to you: a convener, a facilitator, a spiritual leader, a pastor, a guide to the sacred wild—any name you choose! What matters is that you value your own leadership gifts and that you are aware that you aren't the guru.

OUR WILD GATHERING NAME: No, you don't need to call your gathering "church" or "wild"—or anything, for that matter. You might want to play with some names, speak them out loud to the trees, and see how they taste in your mouth. Is there a name for your gathering that feels right, at least to begin?

LISTENING TO YOUR PLACE

Listening deeply to the voices of the wind, leaves, crows, poison ivy, and dried-up riverbeds is the core practice to identify a good place to gather for this work of the Spirit. And of course, there are logistics to consider. Some groups have access to beautiful wild land, which is a gift and privilege. Others live in urban areas, and that, too, is part of the story of nature. Meeting in overly developed places and damaged, desacralized places can be an act of witness, which is part of healing. The crows that roost in the trees planted in parking lots, the hemlock tree growing too tall in a concrete square, the dandelion stubbornly growing through the cracks in the sidewalk: these are touches of wildness persisting in the midst of human domination. These places can become an invitation to witness the land's trauma and allow for the grief we all carry to be shared.

PLACE: What does the land say about the gathering you envision or have already begun? Wander about your town, find the edges, step outside the most obvious spots, and ask, with reverence, the question "Is this a place to gather for wild church? Would you like that?" See what happens. Be prepared to be surprised.

BIOLOGICAL CONTEXT: Who else lives here? Who are the co-congregants? Make a list of some of the beings—fungal, ancestral, geological, vegetal, microbial, furred, hoofed—that would become your preachers and co-congregants as you envision your wild church.

CLIMATE CHANGE: How has the climate crisis impacted your place? In addition to online and library research to find which creatures and plants and trees are threatened by the climate crisis, ask long-term residents how the landscape has changed within their own lifetimes.

WATERSHED: Where do the people and animals find water to survive in your homeplace? Naming your watershed is helpful to remember how connected we are to our landscape.

NATIVE PEOPLES: Whose ancestral tending of this land once defined the human-nature connection for this place? What are their names, histories, and stories? How can you connect personally with people who still live in your region?

POLITICAL HISTORY: What has happened on this land you call home? Is this sacred ground that has been colonized? Have violent battles happened here? Is this a place that once used enslaved peoples to grow particular crops? Has this land been desacralized through industry or human destruction? Note a couple of curiosities to research.

LOGISTICAL CONSIDERATIONS: As you choose a place, consider a few logistics. But don't forget that your most important discernment will come by listening to the land directly.

Access to wildness, in some way, with limited interruption from people is important for transitioning from the concrete world. You'll want enough separateness from other people to privilege the voices of the nonhuman beings. Look for a place that has some access to wild creatures and trees, even edge zones, walkable for just about anyone and easy enough for those carrying chairs and drums. Some ideas:

- *Public Land:* Are there campgrounds, parks, and public trails within a short drive?
- *Private Land:* This can be a good option if you have or can develop relationships with a local retreat center, a land trust, or an owner willing to share.

- *Permits and Cost:* Many parks require permits. Some places require insurance that you may be able to get through a nonprofit partnership.
- *Restrooms:* Not always needed, but it depends on your group. It may be okay in some wilder lands to share the restrooms with the wild animals. Other places, not so much. If you meet for more than two hours or have people with mobility challenges, access to restrooms becomes more important.
- *Shelter:* Do you need a place that is protected from rain or extreme temperatures? Public parks often have picnic shelters that are busy in the summer but empty in the cooler months. Everyone can bring a blanket and huddle close. Is building a fire an option?
- *Distance:* How far away are people willing to drive? Sometimes people say they want to explore different wild areas around a region, but few end up being willing or able to make time for a half-day experience.
- *Parking:* Is it sufficient and safe? Is public transportation available?
- *Accessibility:* Consider your possible group. Accessibility for people with disabilities is important to consider.

FOR OUR FIRST GATHERING, WE WILL MEET: Visit a few spots while holding this question: where do you want to hold your first wild church gathering? You'll know when you find it. Something in your heart and body will say, "Here." Is there a particular place calling to you?

WHEN AND HOW: When and how often do you want to meet? Many wild church leaders begin by meeting monthly or quarterly during seasonal changes.

LISTENING TO YOUR PEOPLE

Who are your people? Even when you think you're the only one in your entire county who feels this call to reconnect spirituality with the living world, you may be surprised to discover you are not alone. You may start your wild church for your own spiritual nurture, as a pathway of your own becoming. But trust us: Lots of people in your community are longing for the same thing. They may not even realize how your wild church is an answer to their own unspoken heart's desire until they hear your vision.

LIST OF PEOPLE: List a few people you can invite to your first wild church gathering.

COMMUNITY: How would you describe the particular constituencies where you live? Are they college students, mystics, people who have left church, churchgoers? You may be surprised at the diversity of people who will be drawn to your gatherings, but it's good to have a sense of your own niche to create your outreach messaging.

TEAM: Who could join you in holding and caring for this vision? Belonging to a team can be more generative than doing it alone. Note, however, that you may need to carry this on your own for a while; people typically need to experience wild church before they are ready to become part of a core team.

DELEGATIONS: A few tasks are important to cover each gathering, including asking someone to:

- Set up a website.
- Collect contact information from all who show up, including phone numbers for last-minute cancellations when there are unsafe weather conditions.
- Maintain communications through emails, social media, a website.
- Stay connected with the movement and other wild churches through the Wild Church Network.
- Greet and direct people from the parking lot.
- Set up the altar.
- Start a fire in the center of your circle (if needed and possible).
- Lead a song or drum circle or dance or tell a story.

AFFILIATIONS AND PARTNERSHIPS: It can be helpful to partner with other local ecological or religious groups. Some wild church leaders work with a local church or several churches. A few have been able to get support from denominations for new church start-ups. More than one leader has connected with a local land trust that lets them borrow their warming hut for gatherings in the winter. List a few possible partners you can approach.

CALLING YOUR PEOPLE: You will have to let people know about your wild church offering. While word of mouth is usually the most effective method, many leaders also use email newsletters, social media, advertisements in their local paper, and apps like Meetup. Posters in coffee shops can be helpful. When communicating with your growing following, remind them to wear comfortable clothing and shoes suitable for the weather and terrain; bring water and a blanket, a folding or backpacking chair, journals, and water. How do you plan to let your community know you're launching a wild church?

PLANNING YOUR GATHERING

Finally, listen to the ideas and stories in this book and consider joining the Wild Church Network to connect with other leaders. Consider your place, your community, and honor your own gifts and vision as you pull together a plan for your first gatherings. Some wild churches start with an Advent or Lenten series as a kind of test. Starting with a few gatherings seems more doable than committing to forever with this new idea. Have a plan, but hold it loosely.

COMMON PRACTICES: What are some of the practices you want to include in your gatherings? You may want to refer to chapters 3–9 for ideas.

UNCOMMON PRACTICES: There are also uncommon practices that are unique to you. For example, some wild churches meet in canoes, some include yoga and tai chi practices, and some have drum circles. Are there any "uncommon" practices that may be unique to who you are / your path?

ORDER OF SERVICE: Finally, order the practices into a format for your first gathering and invite others to lead different aspects of the gathering if possible.

SAMPLE ORDER OF SERVICE: TWO HOUR GATHERING

- Listening for the Welcome of Place (five minutes)
- Drumming / chanting; responsive prayer (ten minutes)
- Embodiment Meditation (five minutes)
- Land Acknowledgement (five minutes)
- Theme / Story introduction (ten minutes)
- Invitation for Wandering (five minutes)
- Solo Sauntering (thirty minutes)
- Circle Sharing (twenty-five minutes)
- Wild Communion (ten minutes)
- Benediction (five minutes)

GRATITUDES AND CONNECTIONS

Enormous gratitude and love to Ollie Loorz and Manne Green for their creative gifts of design and artistry to create the beauty of this field guide. And equally enormous gratitude and love to Alec Loorz for editing this book with such a keen eye for detail and the wisest of hearts. A deep bow to all the wild church leaders out there now who are cocreators in this work: those we know, those we don't know yet, those who are yet to come.

WILDCHURCHNETWORK.COM The Wild Church Network is an organic and emergent organism woven together by people, trees, waters, and lands across the continents, offering support, resources, inspiration, friendship, and a sense of wider belonging to members who have started a wild church or are preparing to. Through weekly and monthly events and online connection platforms, members can connect, share, and learn together. Creating spiritual communities rooted in sacred relationship with the Earth is a countercultural act. The network is here to support you.

WILDSPIRITUALITY.EARTH The Center for Wild Spirituality, with its foundational yearlong intensive program Seminary of the Wild Earth, offers training and support for those who feel called into a new kind of spiritual leadership that reconnects spirituality with the rest of the living world. Offerings include Certifications in Eco-Spirituality, Eco-Spiritual Direction, Wild Spiritual Leadership, and training for new wild church leaders.

THEECOSYSTEM.MN.CO Like a mycelial network of mushrooms that connect trees with resources, we recently implemented a digital platform named The Ecosystem as a gathering place of support, resourcing, inspiration, events, and programs for wild church leaders, people curious about the realignment of spirituality and nature, and students enrolled in the eco-spiritual programs offered by the Center for Wild Spirituality. Anyone is welcome to join.

CONTRIBUTORS

With hearts full of deep gratitude and respect for the following contributors who submitted their acorn gifts of stories, resources, and research, thank you, thank you, thank you! These represent just some of the hundreds of wild churches growing in the rich soil of a spiritual unfolding whose time has come.

MARY ABMA, WILD-EDGE OFFERINGS, BRIGHT'S GROVE, ON. Mary is a member of the Wild Church Network and holds an Eco-Ministry Certificate from Seminary of the Wild. She is an artist, a self-described insect PR person, and an advocate of rewilding using native plant species. Wild-Edge Offerings provides wild church experiences to churches whose members seek to deepen their relationship with God through reconnection with the natural world. Wild church services are held outdoors in respectful relationship with the other-than-human inhabitants of our ecosystems.

BETH AMSBARY, GATHERING GROUND, SEATTLE, WA. The authorship for Gathering Ground's contributions in this book arises from the community itself through Beth. Beth is a seasoned experiential educator and student of spiritual growth who founded the Gathering Ground community in Seattle, where she served as a convener from 2016 to 2023. Beth's journey in meaning-making began in the Christian tradition and has evolved to embrace a multi-belief approach. Gathering Ground provides community for people of many beliefs, on many journeys, to share and forge meaning. We share tools for participating in activities, then reflect, listen, and share our discoveries. Earth's seasons and wisdom guide our year.

SARAH ANDERS, WILD EARTH SPIRITUAL COMMUNITY, WASHINGTON, DC. Sarah is a cofounder and member of Wild Earth Spiritual Community. Wild Earth (WE) gathers outdoors twice a month and offers periodic special events. WE is a participant-centered group aiming for increased relationship with Earth, divine presence, and each other. As participants in the web of creation, we seek to be attentive to the Holy in our midst and invite one another to come home to the sacred ecological ground in which we live. WE functions from a participant-led leadership model.

DIANE ANDERSON, CHAPEL IN THE PINES, WELLESLEY, MA. Diane is a spiritual director and coleads Chapel of the Pines with Michele Ryan. She loves seeing the soft green ferns as they unfurl each spring and the barred owl who silently swoops from branch to branch in the forest surrounding Chapel in the Pines. Chapel in the Pines meets at a recreational town park surrounded by forest to encounter the Sacred in nature through prayer, scripture, and short meditative walks in the forest.

REV. LEANN BLACKERT, WILD CHURCH KAMLOOPS, BC. LeAnn is in ministry with several wild church plants in British Columbia. She makes her home on the unceded ancestral lands of the Syilx Nation in Kelowna. When she's not out wandering the land or sitting under a favorite tree friend, she can be found kayaking in the local lakes or taking long bike rides with her partner or snuggling with her cat. She serves as a member of the steering committee for the Wild Church Network and is a graduate of the Seminary of the Wild.

MINDY BRAUN, WILD JOURNEY, SANTA ROSA, CA. Mindy is a spiritual director and mystic, the director of Journey Center, and founder and facilitator of Wild Journey. Wild Journey is Christ centered, yet all spiritual paths are welcome. Steeped in the Celtic tradition, they gather to remember themselves as part of nature— sacred Earth and sacred souls coming together.

ARND CORTS, WILD CHURCH SAUERLAND, HAGEN, GERMANY. Arnd lives with his wife, Frauke, in Hagen, Germany. He works in the field of organizational development, is a logotherapist / existential analyst in the way of Victor E. Frankl, and teaches tai chi / chi gong. Wild Church Sauerland was founded in 2022 and meets weekly on the edge of the biggest forest area in Europe.

REV. DR. LISA DAHILL, DIRECTOR OF THE CENTER FOR TRANS-FORMATIVE SPIRITUALITY AT HARTFORD INTERNATIONAL UNIVERSITY, HARTFORD, CT. Lisa holds a PhD in Christian Spirituality from the Graduate Theological Union (Berkeley, CA), a Master of Divinity from the Lutheran School of Theology at Chicago, and a Bachelor of Arts in Religion and German from Gustavus Adolphus College (St. Peter, MN). She also studied for a year at the Eberhard-Karls-Universität in Tübingen, Germany. She is past president of the Society for the Study of Christian Spirituality, convener of the Ecology and Liturgy Seminar of the North American Academy of Liturgy, and a rostered clergy member of the New England Synod of the ELCA.

SANDY AND JOHN DRESCHER-LEHMAN, FERNROCK RETREAT WILD CHURCH, GREEN LANE, PA. John and Sandy Drescher-Lehman are retreat hosts for FernRock Retreat Center, along with their dog, Chicory Willow; goats; and chickens. John is a social worker, spiritual director, photographer, and artist who's working with Creator to build the sacred spaces for contemplation on the grounds. Sandy is a pastor, social worker, writer, and spiritual director who loves to use colors and symbols to help build a deeper awareness of God and uses those gifts to help create sacred spaces for contemplation. They offer wild church gatherings at FernRock once a month with time to gather with our intentions of the day, to wander and wonder, offer our presence, and close with an opportunity to share the graces of the day.

REV. LAUREL DYKSTRA, SALAL + CEDAR WATERSHED DISCIPLE-SHIP COMMUNITY, VANCOUVER, BC. Laurel (no pronouns / they / them) is an Anglican priest, environmental activist, and amateur naturalist who lives in the lower Fraser watershed on Coast Salish territory near Vancouver, British Columbia. Laurel leads Salal

+ Cedar Watershed Discipleship Community, a tiny church that worships outdoors and builds skills for climate justice. They have a background in intentional communities and Christian resistance movements and have written books and articles and edited anthologies mostly at the intersection of Bible and social action. They recently authored the book *Wildlife Congregations: A Priest's Year of Gaggles, Colonies and Murders by the Salish Sea.*

COLETTE EATON, WILD CHURCH OF PORTLAND, PORTLAND, OR. Colette is a writer, spiritual contemplative, and pastor of Wild Church of Portland. Her works have appeared in *Ekstasis, Mockingbird,* and *Faith+Lead,* and she writes a regular Substack newsletter, *Courage & Candor,* exploring an evolving faith, contemplation, and the wild church movement. Wild Church of Portland is not about taking a typical church service outdoors and using creation as a backdrop but communing with nature, acknowledging its presence as we would any other person. Taking church outside, beyond the walls and structure of inside church, we invite creation to draw us closer into relationship with Creator God.

KATHY ESCOBAR, FOREST CHURCH, GOLDEN, CO. Kathy is a trained spiritual director, speaker, author, group facilitator, and advocate for people and systematic change in creative ways. She's a cocreator of Forest Church, Golden, CO, a collaborative partnership with Transforming Creatives and The Refuge. As a cofounder and co-pastor of The Refuge, a hub for healing community, social action, and creative collaboration, she loves to be in the nitty-gritty of the human experience.

TAMARA GRENIER, LOWCOUNTRY WILD CHURCH, CHARLESTON / JOHNS ISLAND, SC. Tamara's life has always been infused with a love of and respect for the natural world. In 2013, she was ordained as a Minister of Walking Prayer by the Center for Sacred Studies, a cross-cultural ministry. She considers herself an Earth-based minister, finding spiritual inspiration and connection in nature. She facilitated her first wild church on Nantucket Island in 2021 with a small group of adults and two five-year-old boys and later enrolled in the Wild Church Leadership course. After moving to South Carolina in 2022, she created Lowcountry Wild Church, which is open to all spiritual traditions but is not liturgical. Being present to the Sacred in nature and gathering in unity together and with other-than-human beings is their inspiration.

JIM HALL, WILD EARTH SPIRITUAL COMMUNITY, WASHINGTON, DC. Jim lives in community with others at Dayspring, a small, deeply committed Christian faith community held in the beauty of two hundred acres of woodland, meadow, creeks, and ponds near Washington, DC. Formerly the land of the Piscataway, it is now a place of silent retreat, permaculture gardens, Earth ministries, refugee housing, and prayer. As part of the Church of the Savior for five decades, he practiced medicine at a storefront clinic in the city, then came to Dayspring, where he teaches classes and leads retreats linking soul and nature. He is a member of Wild Earth Spiritual Community.

WENDY JANZEN, BURNING BUSH FOREST CHURCH, KITCHENER–WATERLOO, ON. Wendy is the founder and pastor of Burning Bush Forest Church, a cofounder of the Wild Church Network, and an ordained pastor in Mennonite Church Eastern Canada. She has additional training in eco-ministry and spiritual direction. Burning Bush is a small, experimental worshipping group, individuals who have found ourselves longing for connection with the Divine Spirit in the natural world. We come to nurture our spirits and tend our souls. We come to reconnect with our wild home, our watershed, and the community of creation.

DANA JEFFERSON, ALLEGHENY CATHEDRAL OF THE WILD, HUNTINGDON, PA. Dana is the creator and facilitator of Allegheny Cathedral of the Wild, which was developed to help people connect with their spiritual essence through interaction with nature, in turn creating a love and respect for nature in alignment with Christ consciousness and cosmic sacredness. She is an ordained interfaith minister and a Reiki master. She's a graduate of the Foundation for Shamanic Studies Three-Year Program of Advanced Initiations in Shamanism and Shamanic Healing and has completed a three-year apprenticeship with the Buffalo Trace Society. She has completed coursework in Harner Method Shamanic Counseling and advanced studies in Celtic, Toltec, and Tibetan Shamanism.

LANNI LANTTO, U.P. WILD CHURCH, MARQUETTE, MI. Lanni is the curator for U.P. Wild Church, which has multiple branches across the Upper Peninsula of Michigan on the Great Lakes. In the midst of collecting academic and career achievements with so much vying for her attention, she would always stop to watch the birds. The billboards, the anxieties, the unending pressures, the ways of this world were no match for the authenticity of an encounter with a being that is living proof that God is in our midst. And so her journey continues into the holy unknown with that wild wisdom always as her foundation.

VICTORIA LOORZ, MDIV. OJAI CHURCH OF THE WILD, BELLING-HAM WILD CHURCH, CENTER FOR WILD SPIRITUALITY. Victoria is an eco-spiritual director, founder, and director of the Center for Wild Spirituality and cofounder of the Wild Church Network. She has started and led wild churches in California and Washington and functions more as a wild church apostle these days, delivering workshops and coming up with too many ideas to keep up with herself. Author of *Church of the Wild: How Nature Invites Us into the Sacred*, she is working on her next book with Broadleaf Books, which will be a deeper dive into wild spirituality.

MICHAEL MALLEY, SACRED GROUND WILD CHURCH & SANG-HA, COLUMBUS, OH. Since 2009, Rev. Michael and Ali Malley have led a multi-faith church/sangha, Sacred Ground, in central

Ohio. They meld beneficial teachings of Christianity, Buddhism, and Earth-centered spirituality with the mindfulness teachings of Thich Nhat Hanh. Inspired by the wild church model, Sacred Ground now offers outdoor programs three Sundays per month, with one online broadcast. Services include mindful movement; meditation; Judeo-Christian and Buddhist readings; silent, personal communion with nature; and sharing. Learn more at TheHolyNow.org.

AMY MOFFITT, WILD EARTH SPIRITUAL COMMUNITY, WASHINGTON, DC. It took Amy a long time to realize that music and natural beauty were the things that kept her alive, but blessedly, she did eventually realize it. Amy is fortunate to combine these passions as part of All Joyful Hearts Collective, the unofficial "house band" of Wild Earth Spiritual Community of DC, where she has been active since 2019. She lives in the Washington, DC area with two cats and a view of the sunrise.

CHRISTINE NYGREN, PHD, UNITY CENTER OF PEACE—OUTDOOR SACRED SPACES, CHAPEL HILL, NC. Chris is an artist, shamanic practitioner, and ordained interfaith/interspiritual minister who serves as the Unity Center of Peace Minister of Outdoor Sacred Spaces. The group gathers to deepen connection with nature, self, and all of our relations. She stewards mountain land nearby and enjoys being with her adult daughters and family, who all live in the area.

LEAH RAMPY, CHURCH OF THE WILD TWO RIVERS, SHEPHERDSTOWN, WV. Leah is the founder and convener of Church of the Wild Two Rivers and is an experienced leader of contemplative, Earth-focused retreats and pilgrimages. She is grounded in Christian contemplative, Celtic, and creation spirituality traditions that honor our oneness with Earth as she seeks to learn from other spiritual traditions that chart a path of oneness and compassion.

Gatherings invite the community to come home to the family of nature, to participate in the soul work that offers deeper connection to the Divine, and to take the time to hear the still small voice that is forever seeking us in love.

CARMEN RETZLAFF, FOUNDER AND FORMER PASTOR OF NEW LIFE LUTHERAN CHURCH, DRIPPING SPRINGS, TX. New Life is an outdoor-worshipping community of the ELCA, gathering on twelve acres of beautiful Texas Hill Country land under a giant live oak tree. Candice Coombs is the current pastor of this vibrant congregation. Carmen is now pastor of El Pueblito United Methodist Church, Taos, which worships outdoors with a view of the Sangre de Cristo Mountains in summer months, May to October.

VALERIE LUNA SERRELS, SHENANDOAH VALLEY CHURCH OF THE WILD, BRIDGEWATER, VA. Valerie is the founder and guide of Shenandoah Valley Church of the Wild and a cofounder and director of the Wild Church Network. Her spirituality and the gatherings of Shenandoah Valley Church of the Wild are shaped by her ancestral lineage within the Celtic tradition and the path of the mystics. She approaches wild church as a way to realign ourselves in relationship with an animate world, encounter divine presence in all beings, and awaken the soul as a sacred and critical practice in a time of unmooring and great change. Valerie offers eco-spiritual guidance for individuals and groups and is a graduate of the School for Celtic Consciousness.

REV. DR. WANDA STAHL. Wanda is a spiritual guide, retreat leader, educator, and consultant who has worked in a variety of congregational, denominational, and academic settings. She holds MDiv and STM degrees from Boston University School of Theology and a PhD in Theology and Education from Boston College. Since retiring from Boston University School of Theology in 2022, Wanda has been serving as a program consultant for The BTS Center, an organization focused on cultivating spiritual leadership for a climate-changed world, and on the Leadership Team for Creative Callings, a Lilly Endowment–funded project at Boston University.

JANET STEELE, WILD CHURCH CINCINNATI, CINCINNATI, OH. Janet is a certified biblical storyteller, a certified lay minister in the United Methodist Church, and is currently serving as a team lead for Wild Church Cincinnati, a fresh expression of Clifton United Methodist Church (UMC), a reconciling congregation. During the pandemic, it became apparent that health-care workers were suffering moral injuries due to the nature of the disease and needed spaces for healing. Wild Church Network caught Janet's eye at the same time she stumbled on forest bathing. Wild Church Cincinnati launched in April 2021 in Burnet Woods, an urban forest near local hospitals. It continues to meet monthly and reflects the values of Clifton UMC: a place where all are welcome, no matter what.

KATY TAYLOR, WILD CHURCH PORT TOWNSEND, PORT TOWNSEND, WA. Katy guides Wild Church Port Townsend, affiliated with Quimper Unitarian Universalist Fellowship. She brings her background as an interfaith minister, spiritual coach, and songstress to provide a space to practice remembering our connection with Earth. The Wild Church offers opportunities to gather in and with creation with other folks and with the other beings on this Earth.

GREG TURK, WILD SACRED, SEATTLE WA. Wild Sacred is a spiritual, but not religious, monthly eco-spiritual experience for people seeking community and deep, exquisitely mutual connection with Spirit, land, and the more-than-human world. Together, we are responding to the call to be in sacred, enlivening relationship.

ANDY WADE, BETHEL CONGREGATIONAL CHURCH, WHITE SALMON, WA. Andy is an ordained pastor with the Mennonite Church, currently serving as pastor of Bethel Congregational Church (UCC) in White Salmon, WA. He lives in a multigenerational house in his hometown of Hood River, OR, and thrives outdoors. He can often be found camping in the Gifford Pinchot National

Forest or working in his garden in concert with creation. Andy has helped start and run an emergency shelter for unhoused neighbors, started an organization to assist immigrant neighbors, and, more recently, connected with the local Indigenous community to collaborate on issues of justice and flourishing for all people.

HEATHER WOLFE, WILD CHURCH TAFTSVILLE CHAPEL, WOODSTOCK, VT. Heather is deeply rooted in Vermont, the seventh generation of a family who lives in close relationship with the land. She has grown up in the Mennonite faith tradition and serves as a creation care liaison within that denomination. In 2020, she started a wild church that meets monthly on the land her family stewards. She is a certified Vermont Master Composter; has coauthored a plant-based cookbook, *Sustainable Kitchen*; and is currently attending Seminary of the Wild Earth. Heather feels a spiritual calling to the work of reconciliation, healing the broken relationship between people and creation, as a way of living out love of God and love of neighbor.

MARILYN ZEHR AND SVINDA HEINRICHS, CATHEDRAL OF THE TREES, MAYNOOTH, ON. Marilyn and Svinda are cofounders of Cathedral of the Trees and co-owners of Rise Above Guest House, and both are United Church of Canada ministers. Marilyn is also a forest therapy guide and eco-spiritual director / soul companion. Svinda is a shiatsu therapist and former volunteer firefighter. Both serve their community in various ways, and they find being outdoors is their happy place, reviving their spirits and healing their souls. Cathedral of the Trees gathers in community for a shared experience of wonder in nature, deepening into connection with the elements and other beings with whom we live. The gatherings are open to those who never go to church / temple / synagogue and those who do.

NOTES

1. WILD CHURCH

5   *"constant interactions among individuals suddenly coalesce"*: Margaret Wheatley, *Who Do We Choose to Be?* (Oakland, CA: Berrett-Koehler Publishers, 2023), 273.

6   *"The dead leaves of one culture fall"*: Paul Kingsnorth, "Into the Desert, into the Woods," The Abbey of Misrule, July 7, 2023, accessed March 24, 2024, https://paulkingsnorth.substack.com/p/into-the-desert-into-the-woods.

7   *"The world is not a problem to be solved"*: Llewellyn Vaughan-Lee, *Spiritual Ecology: The Cry of the Earth* (The Point Reyes Station, CA: Golden Sufi Center, 2013), i.

2. GETTING STARTED

16   *"de-center humanity as neither more nor less important"*: Kincentric Leadership Through the Polycrisis Project, "About Kincentric Leadership," accessed March 23, 2024, https://www.kincentricleadership.org/copy-of-about-kincentric-leadership.

19   *"Let the trees find you"*: David Wagoner, "Lost," in *Traveling Light: Collected and New Poems* (Champaign: University of Illinois Press, 1999), 10.

3. ARRIVAL

36   *"To see a World in a Grain"*: William Blake, "Auguries of Innocence," Poetry Foundation, accessed March 22, 2024, https://www.poetryfoundation.org/poems/43650/auguries-of-innocence.

37   *"When we walk on the earth"*: John O'Donohue, *Beauty: The Invisible Embrace* (New York: Harper Perennial, 2005), 35.

42   *"Are you breathing just a little"*: Mary Oliver, ed., "Have You Ever Tried to Enter the Long Black Branches," in *West Wind: Poems and Prose Poems* (New York: Ecco, 1998), 61.

4. ANCESTRAL REVERENCE

51   *"Learning from and with indigenous dialogue partners"*: Lisa E. Dahill, "Rewilding Christian Spirituality: Outdoor Sacraments and the Life of the World," in *Eco-Reformation: Grace and Hope for a Planet*

in Peril, ed. Lisa E. Dahill and James B. Martin-Schramm (Eugene, OR: Wipf & Stock, 2016), 192.

51   *"The land shows bruises"*: Robin Wall Kimmerer, *Braiding Sweetgrass: Indigenous Wisdom, Scientific Knowledge and the Teachings of Plants* (Minneapolis: Milkweed Editions, 2015), 23.

52   *"If we think of territorial acknowledgments as sites"*: Chelsea Vowel, "Beyond Territorial Acknowledgments," âpihtawikosisân, September 23, 2016, accessed March 22, 2024, https://apihta wikosisan.com/2016/09/beyond-territorial-acknowledgments/.

5. WILD RITUALS

66   *Peter Wohlleben shares some startling research:* Peter Wohlleben, *The Heartbeat of Trees: Embracing Our Ancient Bond with Forests and Nature* (London: William Collins Publishers), 74.

7. CONVERSATION WITH THE HOLY WILD

102   *"from idle people who roved about"*: Henry David Thoreau Sauntering, "Walking," *The Atlantic,* June 1862. https://www .theatlantic.com/magazine/archive/1862/06/walking/304674/.

103   *I was sad one day and went for a walk:* Daniel Ladinsky, trans., *Love Poems from God: Twelve Sacred Voices from the East and West,* St. John of the Cross (New York: Penguin Publishing Group, 2002), 323.

104   *The new stories are like:* Martin Shaw, "Small Gods," *Dark Mountain,* no. 7 (April 2015): 17.

8. RE-STORYING OUR PLACE

120   *They need to hear:* Richard Wagamese, *Embers: One Ojibway's Meditations* (Vancouver: Douglas & McIntyre, 2017), 21.

9. OFFERINGS AND BENEDICTION

130   *"What else can you offer"*: Kimmerer, *Braiding Sweetgrass*, 38.